Success in Math

Pre-Algebra

Student Edition

Executive Editor: Barbara Levadi
Market Manager: Sandra Hutchison
Senior Editor: Francie Holder
Editors: Karen Bernhaut, Douglas Falk, Amy Jolin
Editorial Assistant: Kris Shepos-Salvatore
Editorial Consultant: Harriet Slonim
Production Manager: Penny Gibson
Production Editor: Walt Niedner
Interior Design: The Wheetley Company
Electronic Page Production: The Wheetley Company
Cover Design: Pat Smythe

ISBN 0-8359-1182-9
Printed in the United States of America
7 8 9 10 11 12   06 05 04 03 02

1-800-321-3106
www.pearsonlearning.com

Contents

Chapter 1

Introduction to Algebra

◀ OBJECTIVES:

In this chapter, you will learn

- *To use the order of operations to simplify mathematical expressions*
- *To use variables to represent unknown numbers*
- *To write variable expressions for word phrases*
- *To evaluate an expression for a given value of a variable*
- *To identify and use properties of addition and multiplication*
- *To use the Distributive Property of Multiplication over Addition*

Many businesses make use of a computer tool called a spreadsheet for business needs, such as tracking inventory. A spreadsheet is an arrangement of columns and rows called cells which store data. The columns are named by letters and the rows are numbered.

A spreadsheet involves algebraic formulas, which will be studied in this chapter. The spreadsheet below helps a manager keep track of his T-shirt inventory. From this spreadsheet, you can tell that 72 T-shirts were sold on March 2 and 1,707 T-shirts were in stock on March 3.

	A	B	C	D
1	**Date**	**T-shirts Rec'd**	**T-shirts Sold**	**T-shirts in Stock**
2	3/1	2,000	98	1,902
3	3/2		72	1,830
4	3/3		123	1,707
5	3/4		249	1,458
6	3/5		76	1,382
7	3/6		85	1,297

1 • 1 Using Order of Operations

IN THIS LESSON, YOU WILL LEARN
To use the order of operations to simplify mathematical expressions

WORDS TO LEARN
Order of operations *rules for performing mathematical operations in expressions having more than one operation*

Mathematical expression *a combination of numbers and symbols*

Mark called a plumber to fix the kitchen sink. When the plumber finished her work, she wrote on the bill, "Labor: $45 + 2 • $35." Before the plumber could enter the total, Mark said to his brother, Philip, "She's charging us $1,645 for labor!" Philip said, "No, she's charging us $115." Who is correct, Mark or Philip?

New Idea

Mathematicians agree to do mathematical operations in a certain order to simplify mathematical expressions. The rules that describe the order are called rules for the **order of operations** (AWR-duhr uhv ahp-uhr-AY-shuhnz). The order of operations tells you to always multiply or divide first, working from left to right. Then, add or subtract, working from left to right.

A **mathematical expression** (math-uh-MAT-ih-kuhl eks-PREHSH-uhn) is a combination of numbers and symbols, such as $45 + 2 • 35$. To simplify, or perform all the operations in the expression, follow the order of operations.

Examples: Simplify this mathematical expression. $45 + 2 • 35$

$45 + 2 • 35$ ←First multiply.

$45 + 70$ ←Then, add.

115

Philip was right. The plumber charged $115.

Simplify this mathematical expression.
$3 + 12 ÷ 6 + 8 • 3$

$3 + 12 ÷ 6 + 8 • 3$ ←First multiply and divide.

$3 + 2 + 24$ ←Then, add.

29

✓Check Your Understanding

1. What is the first step in simplifying this expression? $15 - 21 \div 3$

_____

_____

Focus on the Idea

To follow the rules for the order of operations to simplify an expression, first do any multiplication or division, working from left to right. Then, do any addition or subtraction, working from left to right.

Practice

Identify the operation to be done first. The first one is done for you.

2. $6 + 12 \div 3$ ___Division___

3. $44 - 3 \cdot 7$ _____

4. $8 + 2 \cdot 5$ _____

5. $12 - 6 \div 2$ _____

6. $20 + 4 \cdot 6$ _____

7. $34 - 14 \div 7$ _____

8. $19 + 10 - 7$ _____

9. $7 + 6 - 2$ _____

Simplify the following mathematical expressions. The first two are done for you.

10. $13 + 11 - 20$ ___4___

11. $26 - 3 + 8$ ___31___

12. $18 \div 9 \cdot 3$ _____

13. $60 \cdot 3 \div 4$ _____

14. $9 \cdot 12 \div 4$ _____

15. $81 \div 9 \cdot 15$ _____

16. $8 + 4 \cdot 6 - 13$ _____

17. $22 - 11 \cdot 2 + 36$ _____

18. $16 + 4 \cdot 2 - 63 \div 7$ _____

19. $42 \div 7 + 3 \cdot 20 - 8$ _____

20. $55 \div 5 + 9 - 3 \cdot 2$ _____

21. $2 \cdot 6 - 6 \div 6 + 15$ _____

Extend the Idea

Parentheses can change what we do first to simplify an expression. Always simplify any part of the expression within parentheses first. If there are parentheses within brackets, simplify the innermost part of the expression first.

Example: Simplify $5 + 8(4 + 2)$.

$5 + 8(4 + 2)$ ←Perform the operation within parentheses.

$5 + 8(6)$ ←Next, multiply.

$5 + 48$ ←Then, add.

53

Some people use the phrase "**Please, My Dear Aunt Sally**" to help them remember the order of operations. The first letters remind them to simplify inside **p**arentheses first, then **m**ultiply and **d**ivide, and then **a**dd and **s**ubtract.

✓Check Your Understanding

22. What is the first step in simplifying this expression?
$100 - [20 - (4 + 1)]$

_____

✓Check the Math

23. Elsa tried to simplify these expressions. Her teacher said her answers were wrong. Simplify each. How did Elsa make her mistakes?

a. $9 + 3(6 - 4)$ **b.** $40 - [6 + 2(7 + 8)]$

_____   _____

_____   _____

_____   _____

_____   _____

_____   _____

Practice

Write all the steps needed to simplify the expression. The first one is done for you.

24. $16 + 2(8 - 3)$ $\underline{16 + 2(5) = 16 + 10 = 26}$

25. $20 - (2 + 9)$ **26.** $15 - (3 + 4)$

_____   _____

27. $10 + 3(5 - 1)$ **28.** $30 + 4(8 - 6)$

_____   _____

29. $40 - 4(9 - 2)$ **30.** $50 - 3(7 + 5)$

_____   _____

31. $(15 - 11)8 \div 4$ **32.** $(10 - 2)7 \div 2$

_____   _____

Simplify. The first one is done for you.

33. $12 + 3(10 - 9) - 6 =$
_____9_____

34. $100 - 4(3 + 7) + 5 =$
_____

35. $90 - 2(6 + 1) + 12 =$
_____

36. $20 + 3(1 + 9) - 10 =$
_____

37. $2(5 - 1) + 10 \div 5 =$
_____

38. $4(6 - 3) + 21 \div 7 =$
_____

39. $25 - [10 - (5 + 2)] =$
_____

40. $13 + [8 - (1 + 3)] =$
_____

41. $3 + [8 - (2 + 3)] =$
_____

42. $12 - [7 - (1 + 2)] =$
_____

Apply the Idea

Elena Rodriguez is a plumber. Her fee is $35 plus $45 per hour of work. Her assistant gets paid $20 per hour.

43. On one job, Ms. Rodriguez worked 4 hours, and her assistant worked 3 hours.

   a. The expression, $35 + 4 \cdot 45 + 3 \cdot 20$, shows the total cost of labor for the plumber and her assistant. Find the value of the expression.

_____

   b. Explain how you got your answer.

_____

44. On a different job, Ms. Rodriguez worked 7 hours, and her assistant worked 9 hours.

   a. Use the expression $35 + 7 \cdot 45 + 9 \cdot 20$ to find the total cost of labor for the plumber and her assistant.

_____

   b. Explain how you got your answer.

_____

Write About It

45. How do the rules for order of operations help you simplify an expression?

_____

_____

⬇1•2 Writing Expressions

⬇ **IN THIS LESSON, YOU WILL LEARN**

To use variables to represent unknown numbers

To write variable expressions for word phrases

WORDS TO LEARN

Variable *a letter used to represent one or more numbers*

Variable expression *an expression that includes numbers, variables, and mathematical symbols*

Roger has signed up 50 volunteers for a walk-a-thon. He needs to sign up still more volunteers before the event. How can you use letters, numbers, and symbols to show the total number of volunteers Roger signs up?

New Idea

The letter v represents how many more volunteers Roger will sign up. The letter v is called a **variable** (VAIR-ee-uh-buhl) because we do not know what number it stands for. Any letter can be used as the variable, but we must always tell what the variable represents. A **variable expression** (VAIR-ee-uh-buhl ehks-PREHSH-uhn) is an expression that includes numbers, variables, and mathematical symbols. A variable expression that stands for the total number of volunteers is $50 + v$.

Variable expressions use the operation symbols $+$, $-$, $\bullet$, and $\div$. Multiplication can also be shown without the multiplication symbol. For example, $5 \bullet a$ can be written as $5a$. Both mean "5 times a."

To write a variable expression for a word phrase:

Step 1 Let a variable stand for the number you do not know. State what the variable stands for.

Step 2 Use the variable and mathematical symbols to show the information in the word phrase.

Examples: Write a variable expression for each word phrase.

Word Phrase—The team lost 10 yards on the play.

Let y stand for the number of yards the team had before the play. Then $y - 10$ stands for the number of yards it has now.

Word Phrase—Barbara bought some used books for $3 each.

Let b stand for the number of books she bought. Then $3b$ stands for the cost of the books.

Focus on the Idea

A variable expression is formed by using a variable for the unknown and inserting symbols as needed.

Practice

Write the letter of the variable expression that matches each description. The first one is done for you.

1. Tom had x books. He lost 1 of them. What variable expression represents the number of books he had left? _____**b**_____

   a. $x + 1$ **b.** $x - 1$ **c.** $1x$ **d.** $x \div 1$

2. June had m magazines. She divided them equally among three friends. What variable expression stands for the total number of magazines she gave each friend? _____

   a. $m + 3$ **b.** $m - 3$ **c.** $m \div 3$ **d.** $3m$

3. Ming bought s pairs of socks. Each pair costs \$2. What variable expression stands for the total cost? _____

   a. $s + \$2$ **b.** $s - \$2$ **c.** $\$2s$ **d.** $\$2 - s$

Write a variable expression for each problem.

4. Joe saved some money. Then he bought a guitar for \$70.

   Let _____ stand for the money Joe saved.

   Then _____ stands for the money he has left.

5. Irene needs some wood trim for her room. It sells for \$4 a foot. Let _____ stand for the amount of the trim Irene needs. Then _____ stands for the total cost.

Apply the Idea

6. Otis gets \$8 an hour for working at the youth center. How can you use a variable expression to stand for the amount of money he earns in a week?

   _____

   _____

Write About It

7. Write a word phrase that could be expressed by "$x - 40$." First decide what x stands for. Explain why your phrase matches the variable expression.

   _____

   _____

◀1•3 Evaluating Expressions

▌In this lesson, you will learn

To evaluate an expression for a given value of a variable

Words to learn

Evaluate *to find the value of a variable expression*

Odetta is selling tickets for $4 each. How can we use a variable expression to show the total number of dollars Odetta receives? How can we use a variable expression to find the total number of dollars Odetta receives if she sells 20 tickets?

New Idea

To **evaluate** (ee-VAL-you-ayt) a variable expression means to find the value of the expression by substituting a number for the variable. The letter t can be used to represent the number of tickets Odetta sells. Since each ticket costs $4, $4t$ represents the total number of dollars she receives. If Odetta sells 20 tickets, then $t = 20$. To find the total number of dollars Odetta receives, we evaluate $4t$.

Example: $4t$ ←Substitute 20 for t.

$4 \cdot 20$ ←Multiply.

$80

So, Odetta receives $80 for the 20 tickets.

The value of a variable expression changes when the value of the variable changes. You can make a table to show the value of a variable expression when different values are used for the variable.

If t is …	1	2	3	10	20	30
then $4t$ …	4	8	12	40	80	120

If x is …	5	6	7	8	9	10
then $2x - 1$ is …	9	11	13	15	17	19

▌Focus on the Idea

To evaluate a variable expression, substitute a given value for the variable in the expression.

Practice

Find the value of each expression if $x = 3$. The first two are done for you.

1. $x + 11$

    $\underline{3 + 11 = 14}$

2. $3x - 5$

    $\underline{3(3) - 5 = 9 - 5 = 4}$

3. $174 + x$

4. $87 - x$

5. $5x - 4$

6. $\dfrac{27}{(x + 6)}$

Complete each table for the given values.

7.

If y is...	1	5	8	12
then $y + 10$ is...	____	____	____	____

8.

If z is...	2	7	10	20
then $3z$ is...	____	____	____	____

9.

If b is...	10	15	17	25
then $b - 5$ is...	____	____	____	____

10.

If x is...	1	2	3	4
then $4x - 3$ is...	____	____	____	____

Apply the Idea

11. A mail-order company adds $2 to the price of an order for handling.

    a. Write an expression that represents the total cost of an order in which the price of the order is c. _____

    b. Find the total cost of the order when $c = 14$. _____

Write About It

12. Explain how to evaluate the expression $75 - 6z$ for $z = 8$.

_____

_____

_____

◀1•4 Using Properties of Operations

At the end of each day, a restaurant manager has to find the total amount of money in the cash register. One day, the restaurant received $275 in cash, $110 in checks, and $325 in credit card charges. The manager added the amounts mentally. How do you think he found the total?

New Idea

In mathematics, we use some rules, called properties, to make our work easier. Often, we can use these properties to compute mentally. You have already used these properties without knowing their names.

The **Commutative Property of Addition** (kuh-MYOOT-uh-tihv PRAHP-uhr-tee uhv uh-DIHSH-uhn) states that the order of the numbers being added does not affect the sum. So, for example,

$$4 + 7 = 11$$
$$7 + 4 = 11$$

You can use groups of pencils or other small objects to show this.

Arrange the 11 pencils in two groups as shown.

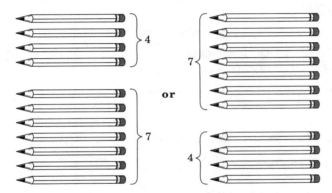

The **Addition Property of 0** (uh-DIHSH-uhn PRAHP-uhr-tee uhv ZIHR-oh) states that the sum of 0 and any number is that number. So, if 0 pencils are added to the 11, there are still 11. $11 + 0 = 11$

Now, make three groups with the 11 pencils, arranging them as shown.

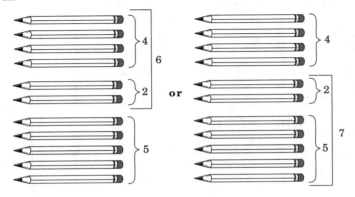

Notice that the way you group the pencils does not change the sum. The **Associative Property of Addition** (uh-SOH-shee-ayt-ive PRAHP-uhr-tee uhv uh-DIHSH-uhn) states that the order in which the numbers are grouped does not affect the sum. So, $(4 + 2) + 5 = 11$ and $4 + (2 + 5) = 11$.

The properties of addition can be used to find sums mentally. The restaurant manager could have thought:

$275 + $110 + $325
($275 + $325) + $110
$600 + $110
$710

The manager's total for the day was $710.

✓ *Check the Math*

1. Which properties of addition could be applied to make the problem above easier to solve mentally? Explain your answer.

_____

_____

◀ Focus on the Idea

Numbers can be added in any order. Numbers can be grouped in any order when they are being added. The sum of 0 and a number is that number.

Practice

Tell which property of addition is shown. The first one is done for you.

2. $12 + 17 = 17 + 12$ ___Commutative Property of Addition___

3. $4 + (2 + 7) = (4 + 2) + 7$ _____

4. $13 + 47 = 47 + 13$ _____

5. $20 + (75 + 25) = (20 + 75) + 25$ _____

6. $91 + 0 = 91$ _____

Find the sum. Use the properties to make your work easier. The first one is done for you.

7. $1 + 235 + 99$ $= (1 + 99) + 235$
$= 100 + 235$
$= 335$

8. $25 + 57 + 75$ _____
_____
_____

9. $2 + 19 + 18$ _____

10. $30 + 0 + 70$ _____
_____
_____

Extend the Idea

Arrange two groups of 8 pencils, as shown.

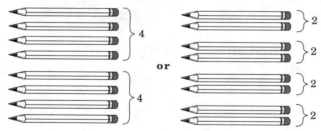

The **Commutative Property of Multiplication** (kuh-MYOOT-uh-tihv PRAHP-uhr-tee uhv uh-DIHSH-uhn) states that the order in which the numbers are multiplied does not affect the product. So, $2 \cdot 4 = 8$ and $4 \cdot 2 = 8$.

The **Associative Property of Multiplication** (uh-SOH-shee-ayt-ive PRAHP-uhr-tee uhv mul-tuh-plih-KAY-shuhn) states that the way in which numbers are grouped does not affect the product. So, for example, $(2 \cdot 3) \cdot 3 = 18$ and $2 \cdot (3 \cdot 3) = 18$.

The **Multiplication Property of 1** (mul-tuh-plih-KAY-shuhn PRAHP-uhr-tee uhv wun) states that any number multiplied by 1 is not changed. If there is 1 group of 6 pencils, there are 6 pencils. So, $1 \cdot 6 = 6$.

The **Multiplication Property of 0** (mul-tuh-plih-KAY-shuhn PRAHP-uhr-tee uhv ZIHR-oh) states that any number multiplied by 0 has a product of zero. If there are 0 groups of 5 pencils, there are 0 pencils. So, 0 • 5 = 0.

✓ *Check Your Understanding*

11. Which property of multiplication could you use to find the product of 5 • (13 • 2) easily? How could you use that property?

_____

Practice

Tell which property of multiplication is shown. The first one is done for you.

12. 5 • (2 • 16) = (5 • 2) • 16 ___Associative Property___

13. 21 • 43 = 43 • 21 _____

14. 0 • 486 = 0 _____

15. (4 • 16) • 10 = 4 • (16 • 10) _____

16. 210 • 1 = 210 _____

Find the product. Use the properties to make your work easier. The first one is done for you.

17. 2 • (50 • 24)   18. (12 • 25) • 4   19. 5 • (7 • 2)

    = (2 • 50) • 24   _____   _____

    = (100 • 24)   _____   _____

    = 2,400   _____   _____

Apply the Idea

20. Gloria needs to find the cost of carpeting a room. To do this, she must multiply the length of the room by the width, then by the cost of one square yard of carpeting. How can she multiply mentally to find the cost of carpeting her 5 yd by 3 yd bedroom with carpeting that costs $20 per square yard?

_____

✏ Write About It

21. Simplify the expressions (48 ÷ 24) ÷ 2 and 48 ÷ (24 ÷ 2). Tell whether or not the associative property helps you simplify.

_____

_____

_____

Using the Distributive Property of Multiplication Over Addition

◀ **IN THIS LESSON, YOU WILL LEARN**

To use the Distributive Property of Multiplication Over Addition

WORDS TO LEARN

Distributive Property of Multiplication Over Addition
states that there are two ways to find the product of a number and a sum

Solar Electronics sells solar batteries for $30 a dozen. How was the total due determined in each bill shown here?

Solar Electronics			
Date: June 10			
Bill to Karen Jones			
Item	Quantity A	Quantity B	Unit Price
Batteries	3 doz	4 doz	$30/doz
		Total Due	$210

Solar Electronics			
Date: August 8			
Bill to Peter Thomas			
Item	Quantity	Unit Price	Subtotal
Batteries	3 doz	$30/doz	$ 90
Batteries	4 doz	$30/doz	$120
		Total Due	$210

New Idea

The **Distributive Property of Multiplication Over Addition** (dih-STRIHB-yoo-tihv PRAHP-uhr-tee uhv mul-tuh-plih-KAY-shuhn OH-vuhr uh-DIHSH-uhn) states that the product of a sum equals the sum of the products.

The quantities, costs, and totals are the same on both of the Solar Electronics bills.

On the June 10 bill:
$(3 + 4) \cdot 30$
    $7 \cdot 30$ ← Product of Sum
    210

On the August 8 bill:
$(3 \cdot 30) + (4 \cdot 30)$
        $90 + 120$ ← Sum of Products
            210

Since the two bills are both for the same quantities at the same unit price, one was determined as the product of a sum and the other as the sum of two products.

Example: Use the Distributive Property of Multiplication Over Addition to find the product. $24 \cdot 312$

Multiply 312 by 24.

$$
\begin{array}{r}
312 \\
\times\ 24 \\
\hline
1{,}248 \\
6{,}240 \\
\hline
7{,}488
\end{array}
$$

←— 24 = 20 + 4
←— 4 × 312
←— 20 × 312
←— Add.

✓Check the Math

1. Which example, a or b, shows the Distributive Property of Multiplication Over Addition? _____

   a. $2 + (3 + 5) = (2 + 3) + 5$

   b. $5 \cdot (6 + 3) = (5 \cdot 6) + (5 \cdot 3)$

◤ Focus on the Idea

The Distributive Property of Multiplication Over Addition states that you can use two methods to find the product of a number and a sum.
For example, 2 (4 + 6) = 2 (4) + 2 (6).

Practice

Write *yes* if the example shows the Distributive Property of Multiplication Over Addition. Write *no* if it does not.

2. $5 + (4 \cdot 3) = 5 + 4 \cdot 3$ _____

3. $8 \cdot (2 + 9) = (8 \cdot 2) + (8 \cdot 9)$ _____

4. $7 \cdot (6 \cdot 4) = (7 \cdot 6) \cdot 4$ _____

Underline the part of the equation that is easier to work with. Then simplify.

5. $9 \cdot (4 + 6) = (9 \cdot 4) + (9 \cdot 6)$ _____

6. $7 \cdot (3 + 8) = (7 \cdot 3) + (7 \cdot 8)$ _____

7. $16 \cdot (10 + 3) = (16 \cdot 10) + (16 \cdot 3)$ _____

8. $25 \cdot (30 + 2) = (25 \cdot 30) + (25 \cdot 2)$ _____

9. $256 \cdot (100 + 2) = (256 \cdot 100) + (256 \cdot 2)$ _____

Apply the Idea

10. Mario earns $7 per hour at a fast-food restaurant. He worked 4 hours on Friday and 8 hours on Saturday. How much did he earn for both days? _____

✎ Write About It

11. Use the Distributive Property of Multiplication Over Addition to rewrite the expression $(7 \cdot 22) + (7 \cdot 78)$. Simplify your expression. Tell why rewriting it made simplifying easy.

Chapter 1   Review

In This Chapter, You Have Learned
- To use the order of operations to simplify mathematical expressions
- To write and evaluate variable expressions
- To identify and use the Commutative and Associative properties of Addition and Multiplication
- To identify and use the Distributive Property of Multiplication Over Addition

Words You Know

Choose the letter of the phrase or expression in Column 2 that best matches the word or phrase in Column 1.

Column 1	Column 2
1. variable expression _____	**a.** $5(4 + 3) = 5(4) + 5(3)$
2. evaluate _____	**b.** $3a - 17$
3. order of operations _____	**c.** find the value of an expression
4. mathematical expression _____	**d.** rules for getting an answer when an expression has more than one operation
5. Commutative Property of Addition _____	
6. Associative Property of Multiplication _____	**e.** $594 + 608 = 608 + 594$
	f. $(3 \cdot 5) \cdot 9 = 3 \cdot (5 \cdot 9)$
7. Multiplication Property of 0 _____	**g.** $0 \cdot 35 = 0$
8. Distributive Property of Multiplication Over Addition _____	**h.** a combination of numbers and symbols

More Practice

Simplify.

9. $8(7 - 4)$ _____

10. $41 - 3 \cdot 5 + 4$ _____

11. $25 - (3 + 4)$ _____

12. $63 - (12 + 9) + 6$ _____

13. $42 - [16 \div (4 + 4)]$ _____

14. $108 - [42 - (10 - 3)]$ _____

Write the letter of the variable expression that matches each description.

15. Lucinda had c post cards. She mailed 15 of them. What variable expression stands for the number of cards she has left? _____

    a. $15c$ **b.** $c - 15$ **c.** $15 - c$ **d.** $c + 15$

16. Ned buys s shirts. Each shirt costs \$19. What variable expression stands for the total cost? _____

    a. $19 + s$ **b.** $s - 19$ **c.** $19s$ **d.** $s \div 19$

Find the value of each expression if $m = 9$.

17. $m + 11 = $ _____   **18.** $3m$ _____

19. $m - 4$ _____   **20.** $2m - 1$ _____

Tell which property of addition or multiplication is shown.

21. $3 + 7 = 7 + 3$ _____

22. $8(3 + 1) = (8 \cdot 3) + (8 \cdot 1)$ _____

23. $9 \cdot 1 = 9$ _____

24. $3 \cdot (2 \cdot 8) = (3 \cdot 2) \cdot 8$ _____

25. $46 \cdot 0 = 0$ _____

26. $8 \cdot 5 = 5 \cdot 8$ _____

Tell which property you can use to make simplifying the expression easy. Then rewrite the expression, and simplify.

27. $5 \cdot (11 \cdot 6)$ _____

28. $(8 \cdot 32) + (8 \cdot 18)$ _____

Problems You Can Solve

29. A film editor charges \$60 per hour.

    a. Write an expression that tells the total amount the film editor charges if he works h hours. _____

    b. Find the total amount he charges for 7 hours of work.

    _____

30. Bruce earns \$6 per hour. He worked 5 hours on Saturday and 7 hours on Sunday. How much did he earn for both days?

_____

31. **For Your Portfolio** Think of a real-life situation that could be described by using a variable expression. Write the variable expression, telling what the variable represents. Then, on a separate sheet of paper, make a table in which you evaluate the expression for other values of the variable.

Chapter 1   Practice Test

Simplify.

1. $6(9 + 2)$ _____

2. $19 - 2 \cdot 4 + 4$ _____

3. $35 - (2 + 8)$ _____

4. $51 - (31 + 9)$ _____

5. $54 - [24 \div (4 + 2)]$ _____

6. $65 - [15 - (10 - 8)]$ _____

Write the letter of the variable expression that matches each description.

7. Uri works 5 hours on Saturday. She works n hours on Sunday. What variable expression stands for the total number of hours she works during the two days?
   _____

   a. $5n$ **b.** $n \div 5$ **c.** $n - 5$ **d.** $5 + n$

8. Maro made 20 cookies. She divided them equally among n friends. What variable expression stands for the number of cookies each friend received?
   _____

   a. $20 + n$ **b.** $20n$ **c.** $20 \cdot n$ **d.** $20 \div n$

Find the value of each expression if $x = 8$.

9. $x + 34$ _____

10. $6x$ _____

11. $x - 3$ _____

12. $50 \div (x + 2)$ _____

Tell which property of addition or multiplication is shown.

13. $4 \cdot 9 = 9 \cdot 4$ _____

14. $5(2 + 9) = (5 \cdot 2) + (5 \cdot 9)$ _____

15. $7 + 0 = 7$ _____

16. $1 \cdot 23 = 23$ _____

17. $5 \cdot (6 \cdot 8) = (5 \cdot 6) \cdot 8$ _____

18. $22 \cdot 0 = 0$ _____

Tell which property you can use to make simplifying the expression easier. Then rewrite the expression and simplify.

19. $25 \cdot (23 \cdot 4)$ _____

20. $(7 \cdot 16) + (7 \cdot 4)$ _____

Chapter 2

Solving Equations with Whole Numbers

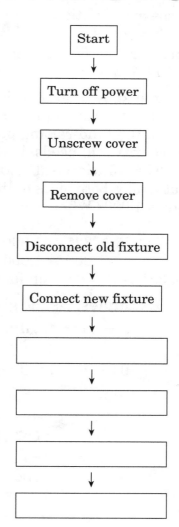

OBJECTIVES:

In this chapter, you will learn

- *To recognize equations*
- *To recognize the solution to an equation*
- *To solve equations using addition*
- *To solve equations using subtraction*
- *To solve equations using multiplication*
- *To solve equations using division*

To make an electrical repair, it is important to follow safety rules. For example, before changing a light fixture, you must turn off the electrical power to that fixture. Then, after you have installed the fixture, you must remember to turn the power back on.

A flowchart is a diagram that outlines a way of doing something. The beginning of a flowchart for changing a light fixture is shown at the right.

At this point, you must retrace your steps to finish the job. Complete the flow chart to show how you would do it.

Start
↓
Turn off power
↓
Unscrew cover
↓
Remove cover
↓
Disconnect old fixture
↓
Connect new fixture
↓

▶**IN THIS LESSON, YOU WILL LEARN**

To recognize equations

To recognize the solution to an equation

WORDS TO LEARN

Equation *a statement that two expressions are equal*

Solution *the value of the variable that makes an equation true*

At a charity fund-raising party, $675 was raised. The goal is $1,000. To reach the goal, how much more money does the charity need?

New Idea

An **equation** (ee-KWAY-zhuhn) is a statement that two expressions are equal.

These are equations:

$$3 + y = 4 \qquad x + 11 = 15 \qquad 2n - 5 = 1$$

These are not equations:

$$14 - 6 = 9 \qquad 8 = 18 \qquad 8 \div 4 = 0$$

You know that a variable can stand for a number in a problem. An equation can stand for the entire problem.

In the fund-raising problem, let x stand for the number of dollars the charity still needs. Use $675 + x = 1,000$ to express the problem.

The **solution** (suh-LOO-shuhn) to an equation is a value for a variable that makes both sides of the equation equal. What number added to 675 equals 1,000? When you substitute 325 for x, you get a true statement.

$$675 + x = 1,000 \qquad \leftarrow \text{Substitute 325 for } x.$$
$$675 + 325 = 1,000 \qquad \leftarrow \text{Both sides of the equation equal 1,000.}$$
$$1,000 = 1,000$$

So, 325 is the solution for $675 + x = 1,000$.

Examples: Is the given number the solution for the equation?

$x + 37 = 49$; if $x = 11$ — No, 11 is not the solution because $11 + 37 = 49$ is not true.

$94 - v = 74$; if $v = 20$ — Yes, 20 is the solution because $94 - 20 = 74$ is true.

▶## Focus on the Idea

An equation is a statement that two expressions are equal. To solve an equation means to find a number for the variable that makes the equation true.

Practice

Is the number given for the variable the solution of the equation? Write *yes* or *no*. The first two are done for you.

1. $x + 11 = 32$; if $x = 3$ <u>no; 3 + 11 = 32 is not true</u>
2. $y - 20 = 30$; if $y = 50$ <u>yes; 50 - 20 = 30 is true</u>
3. $c + 1 = 7$; if $c = 6$ _____
4. $m - 8 = 2$; if $m = 10$ _____
5. $r + 9 = 11$; if $r = 4$ _____
6. $t - 42 = 10$; if $t = 52$ _____

Write *a*, *b*, or *c*, to tell which value for the variable is the solution of the equation.

7. $x + 6 = 14$ **a.** $x = 6$ **b.** $x = 8$ **c.** $x = 9$ _____
8. $m - 12 = 20$ **a.** $m = 8$ **b.** $m = 12$ **c.** $m = 32$ _____
9. $d - 7 = 9$ **a.** $d = 2$ **b.** $d = 16$ **c.** $d = 17$ _____
10. $y + 8 = 15$ **a.** $y = 7$ **b.** $y = 8$ **c.** $y = 23$ _____
11. $2x = 28$ **a.** $x = 14$ **b.** $x = 30$ **c.** $x = 56$ _____
12. $\frac{w}{5} = 10$ **a.** $w = 2$ **b.** $w = 5$ **c.** $w = 50$ _____

Apply the Idea

A company pays Stacey $0.20 for each piece of equipment she tests. Today, she earned $36. She is not sure how many pieces of equipment she tested. Let p stand for the number of pieces she tested.

13. Which equation could Stacey use to find how many pieces of equipment she tested? _____

     a. $0.20 + p = 36$ **b.** $0.20 - p = 36$ **c.** $0.20\,p = 36$

14. What is the solution to the equation you chose? _____

15. Write an equation Stacey could use to find the number of pieces she tested on the day she earned $34.60. Then solve the equation. _____

Write About It

16. Write about a time in which you received an amount of money, then spent part of it. Write an equation that represents this. Then solve the equation.

_____

_____

Solving Equations
by Adding

IN THIS LESSON, YOU WILL LEARN

To solve equations using addition

WORDS TO LEARN

Addition Property of Equality *a rule stating that the same number can be added to each side of an equation*

Inverse operations *mathematical operations that reverse, or "undo" each other*

When Felipe received his first paycheck, it was for $437. He had deductions of $142, but Felipe wanted to figure out how much his salary was before the deductions. How could he determine this?

New Idea

The **Addition Property of Equality** (uh-DIHSH-uhn PRAHP-uhr-tee uhv ee-KWAWL-uh-tee) is a rule stating that if you add the same number to each side of an equation, the two sides remain equal. Addition and subtraction are **inverse operations** (ihn-VERS ahp-uhr-AY-shuhnz). Inverse operations "undo" each other.

Example: Get 8 counters. Place them in two groups of 4 on a sheet of paper. Write an equal sign between the two groups.

$$\square\square \atop \square\square = \square\square \atop \square\square$$

The counters show that $4 = 4$.

Add 2 more counters to the group on the left. Now, what must you do to keep the two sides equal?

If you add 2 more counters to the group on the right, the two groups are again equal. Express this as:

$$4 + 2 = 4 + 2$$

Felipe's problem can be solved with this equation. The variable x stands for his salary before deductions:

$$x - 142 = 437$$

The equation says that "when 142 is subtracted from x, the difference is 437." To find his salary before deductions were taken, you must "undo" the subtraction.

$$x - 142 = 437 \quad \leftarrow \text{Equation}$$
$$x - 142 + 142 = 437 + 142 \quad \leftarrow \text{Add 142 to both sides of the equation to "undo" subtracting 142.}$$
$$x = 579$$

Felipe's salary before deductions are taken is $579.

✓ Check Your Understanding

1. You have two equal groups of counters. If you add 5 to one group, what must you do to keep the two groups equal?

_____

◢ Focus on the Idea

The Addition Property of Equality states that if the same number is added to each side of an equation, the two sides remain equal. An inverse operation can be used to solve equations.

Practice

Write a new equation using the Addition Property of Equality. The first one is done for you.

2. Add 3 to each side.
   $a = 10$

   $\underline{\quad a + 3 = 10 + 3 \quad}$

   $\underline{\quad a + 3 = 13 \quad}$

3. Add 20 to each side.
   $b = 15$

   _____

   _____

4. Add 99 to each side.
   $r = 1$

   _____

   _____

5. Add 17 to each side.
   $s = 16$

   _____

   _____

6. Add 4 to each side.
   $x = 5$

   _____

   _____

7. Add 1 to each side.
   $y = 7$

   _____

   _____

8. Add 10 to each side.
   $z = 96$

   _____

   _____

9. Add 23 to each side.
   $c = 39$

   _____

   _____

What is the inverse operation?

10. Subtract 123 _____

11. Add 41 _____

12. Add 25 _____

13. Subtract 19 _____

14. Add 6 _____

15. Subtract 8 _____

Write a new equation using an inverse operation.

16. $w - 14 = 32$

   _____

17. $z - 8 = 15$

   _____

18. $t - 20 = 48$

   _____

19. $h - 100 = 431$

   _____

Extend the Idea

You can think of inverse operations as working backwards or as doing a job from end to beginning.

At work, Francine seals salad dressing in single packets for restaurants. Then, she places 100 packets in a box and seals the box. When a restaurant gets a box, the restaurant manager must undo Francine's work. The manager must first unseal the box, then unseal a packet.

We can apply this "undoing" to an equation.

Example: Solve the equation.

$$y - 21 = 37 \qquad \leftarrow \text{Equation}$$
$$y - 21 + 21 = 37 + 21 \qquad \leftarrow \text{Add 21 to both sides to}$$
$$\text{"undo" subtracting 21.}$$
$$y = 58$$

✓Check the Math

20. Andre said that if $x - 24 = 90$, x is less than 90. Is he correct? Explain your answer.

   _____

Practice

Complete to solve the equation. The first one is done for you.

21. $x - 13 = 76$

   $x - 13 + 13 = 76 + \underline{\quad 13 \quad}$

   $x = \underline{\quad 89 \quad}$

22. $a - 45 = 62$

   $a - 45 + 45 = 62 + \underline{\qquad\qquad}$

   $a = \underline{\qquad\qquad}$

23.
$$g - 11 = 10$$
$$g - 11 + 11 = 10 + \underline{\hspace{1.5in}}$$
$$g = \underline{\hspace{1.5in}}$$

24.
$$x - 56 = 78$$
$$x - 56 + \underline{\hspace{0.8in}} = 78 + \underline{\hspace{0.8in}}$$
$$x = \underline{\hspace{1.5in}}$$

Solve each equation.

25. $x - 65 = 93$

26. $x - 121 = 79$

27. $x - 24 = 14$

28. $x - 37 = 45$

29. $x - 83 = 95$

30. $x - 91 = 48$

31. $x - 63 = 41$

32. $x - 33 = 66$

Apply the Idea

33. Phil withdraws $80 from his checking account at an ATM. The receipt shows that the new balance in his account is $4,029. Write and solve an equation that shows how much money he had in his account before he withdrew the $80.

_____

Write About It

34. Explain how you can figure out whether or not your solution to an equation is correct.

_____

_____

_____

➤2•3 Solving Equations by Subtracting

◄ **IN THIS LESSON, YOU WILL LEARN**

To solve equations using subtraction

WORDS TO LEARN

Check the Solution *substituting a number or numbers for the variable or variables in the original equation*

Larry needs 240 points to earn a B in history. He has earned 173 points. How many more points does he need?

New Idea

Make two groups of counters with 5 in a group. Place them on a sheet of paper. Write an equal sign between the groups.

The counters show that $5 = 5$.

Take two counters away from one group. What must you do to keep the two groups equal?

If you subtract 2 counters from the other group, then the two groups are again equal. Express this as:

$$5 - 2 = 5 - 2$$

Example: To solve Larry's problem, write the equation $x + 173 = 240$, where x stands for points he still needs.

$$x + 173 = 240 \qquad \leftarrow \text{Equation}$$

$$x + 173 - 173 = 240 - 173 \qquad \leftarrow \text{Subtract 173 from both sides of the equation to "undo" adding 173.}$$

$$x = 67$$

Larry needs 67 more points to get a B.

Check the solution (chehk theh soe-LOO-shuhn), 67, by substituting it for the variable in the original equation. If both sides of the equation remain equal, the answer is correct. (Note: the symbol $\stackrel{?}{=}$ is used in a check when you do not know if the left and right sides of an equation are equal.)

$$x + 173 = 240 \qquad \leftarrow \text{Substitute 67 for } x.$$

$$67 + 173 \stackrel{?}{=} 240 \qquad \leftarrow \text{Simplify.}$$

$$240 = 240 \qquad \leftarrow \text{Both sides remain equal.}$$

So, 67 is the correct solution.

Focus on the Idea

An addition equation is solved by subtracting the same amount from both sides of the equation.

Practice

Solve each equation. The first one is done for you.

1. $b + 7 = 15$
    $b + 7 - 7 = 15 - 7$
    $b = 8$

2. $m + 9 = 11$

3. $c + 4 = 19$

4. $x + 20 = 30$

5. $e + 25 = 51$

6. $f + 24 = 30$

7. $k + 37 = 72$

8. $l + 76 = 91$

9. $o + 32 = 92$

10. $p - 32 = 98$

Apply the Idea

11. Maria is a paramedic. She has pledged 200 hours to the volunteer ambulance corps. So far, she has given 128 hours. How many more hours does she have to give?

    a. Solve the equation. $h + 128 = 200$ _____

    b. What does the solution to the equation tell you?

    _____

✏ Write About It

12. Choose any number from 1 to 100.

    a. Write two different equations for which your number is the solution. _____

    b. Explain how you can be sure that your number is the solution to each equation.

    _____

    _____

➤2•4 Solving Equations by Multiplying

IN THIS LESSON, YOU WILL LEARN
To solve equations using multiplication

WORDS TO LEARN
Multiplication Property of Equality *a rule stating that if each side of an equation is multiplied by the same number, the sides are still equal*

Six friends go on a trip. They share the expenses for tolls and gasoline equally. Each friend pays $21 for the trip. How much do the tolls and gasoline cost all together?

New Idea

Put counters in two groups of 3 each. Write an equal sign between them. Then write the equation that this represents.

☐☐☐ = ☐☐☐ $3 = 3$

Now, double the number of counters on each side of the equal sign. Now you can write:

$$\frac{\square\square\square}{\square\square\square} = \frac{\square\square\square}{\square\square\square}$$ $2 \cdot 3 = 2 \cdot 3$
$6 = 6$

The **Multiplication Property of Equality** (mul-tuh-plih-KAY-shun PRAHP-uhr-tee uhv ee-KWAWL-uh-tee) states that if you multiply each side of an equation by the same number, the sides will still be equal.

Multiplication is the inverse operation for division. Multiplying by 3 (or $\frac{3}{1}$) "undoes" dividing by 3.

Example: Use the Multiplication Property to solve $\frac{x}{3} = 5$.

$\frac{x}{3} = 5$ ← Equation

$\frac{x}{3} \cdot \frac{3}{1} = 5 \cdot 3$ ← Multiply each side by 3.

$x = 15$

Focus on the Idea
To solve an equation involving division, multiply both sides of the equation by the same number.

Practice

Solve each equation. The first one is done for you.

1. $\frac{r}{15} = 10$

    $\frac{r}{5} \cdot 15 = 10 \cdot 15$

    $r = 150$

2. $\frac{g}{7} = 21$

3. $\frac{y}{7} = 3$

4. $\frac{i}{10} = 42$

5. $\frac{w}{4} = 12$

6. $\frac{d}{20} = 34$

7. $\frac{a}{6} = 15$

8. $\frac{k}{21} = 76$

9. $\frac{b}{8} = 23$

10. $\frac{s}{9} = 25$

11. $\frac{h}{5} = 100$

12. $\frac{x}{3} = 33$

Apply the Idea

13. Refer to the problem about the friends' trip on page 28. Write and solve an equation to determine the total cost of tolls and gasoline. _____

14. Mrs. Wong is paying for new office equipment in three equal payments. Each payment is $345. Write and solve an equation to find the total cost of the equipment.

    _____

Write About It

15. How can you be sure that multiplication and division are inverse operations? Explain your answer. Give examples.

    _____

    _____

    _____

►2•5 Solving Equations by Dividing

IN THIS LESSON, YOU WILL LEARN

To solve equations by using division

WORDS TO LEARN

Division Property of Equality *a rule stating that if each side of an equation is divided by the same nonzero number, the sides are still equal*

Tickets to a local basketball game cost $5 each. The boosters club has $75 to buy tickets to the game for children in the Big Brothers and Sisters Program. How many tickets can the club buy?

New Idea

Put counters in two groups of 15 each. Put the groups on a sheet of paper and write an equal sign between them. The counters show that $15 = 15$.

Divide each group into three equal sets. Express this as: $\frac{15}{3} = \frac{15}{3}$ Simplified, the equation for the new arrangement is $5 = 5$.

The **Division of Property of Equality** states that when each side of an equation is divided by the same number, the sides remain equal.

Example: The equation for the basketball ticket problem is $5x = 75$. The variable x stands for the number of tickets that can be bought. Remember that $5x$ means 5 "times" x.

$$5x = 75 \leftarrow \text{Equation}$$
$$\frac{5x}{5} = \frac{75}{5} \leftarrow \text{Divide each side by 5.}$$
$$x = 15$$

The club can buy 15 tickets to the game.
To check your solution, substitute 15 for x in the equation.

$$5 \cdot 15 \stackrel{?}{=} 75$$
$$75 = 75 \qquad \leftarrow \text{The two sides of the equation are equal.}$$

So, 15 is the correct solution.

✓Check Your Understanding

1. How would you solve the equation $9x = 45$?

Focus on the Idea

To solve an equation involving multiplication, divide each side of the equation by the same number.

Practice

Solve each equation. The first one is done for you.

2. $2x = 78$

$\frac{2x}{2} = \frac{78}{2}$

$x = 39$

3. $3x = 36$

4. $6x = 18$

5. $7x = 42$

6. $4a = 76$

7. $8b = 88$

8. $5c = 175$

9. $6d = 438$

10. $10g = 450$

11. $20h = 680$

12. $25k = 275$

13. $50l = 850$

Extend the Idea

To solve an equation, you must first decide whether to add, subtract, multiply, or divide.

The equation $x + 4 = 15$ says, "When 4 is added to x, the result is 15." To solve the equation, subtract 4 from each side.

$x + 4 = 15$

$x + 4 - 4 = 15 - 4$

$x = 11$

The equation $3x = 75$ says, "When x is multiplied by 3, the result is 75." To solve the equation, divide each side by 3.

$3x = 75$

$\frac{3x}{3} = \frac{75}{3}$

$x = 25$

The equation $x - 24 = 73$ says, "When 24 is subtracted from x, the result is 73." To solve the equation, add 24 to each side.

$$x - 24 = 73$$
$$x - 24 + 24 = 73 + 24$$
$$x = 97$$

The equation $\frac{x}{5} = 14$ says, "When x is divided by 5, the result is 14." To solve the equation, multiply each side by 5.

$$\frac{x}{5} = 14$$
$$\frac{x}{5} \cdot 5 = 14 \cdot 5$$
$$x = 70$$

✓Check the Math

14. Hinda solved the equation $x - 17 = 128$. Her solution was 111. Is 111 the correct solution? How might Hinda have found it?

_____

_____

Practice

Explain each equation. The first one has been done for you.

15. $x - 21 = 70$ <u>21 has been subtracted from x to get 70</u>

16. $6x = 60$ _____

17. $\frac{x}{2} = 18$ _____

18. $x + 9 = 34$ _____

19. $4x = 72$ _____

Solve each equation. The first one has been done for you.

20. $a + 6 = 11$
$$a + 6 - 6 = 11 - 6$$
$$a = 5$$

21. $g + 11 = 48$

22. $h - 3 = 78$

23. $3i = 27$

24. $\frac{k}{5} = 25$

25. $l + 45 = 70$

26. $12m = 60$

27. $n - 17 = 94$

28. $\frac{o}{7} = 35$

29. $d - 71 = 80$ **30.** $8e = 72$ **31.** $\frac{f}{7} = 11$

Write the letter of the equation you can use to solve the problem.

32. Steve bought tickets for the movies. Each ticket cost $6. He paid $72. How many tickets did he buy? _____

   a. $x + 6 = 72$ **b.** $\frac{x}{6} = 72$ **c.** $6x = 72$

33. Laura works in a department store. She earned $420 last week working 35 hours. How much is that per hour? _____

   a. $35x = 420$ **b.** $\frac{x}{35} = 420$ **c.** $x + 35 = 420$

34. Nina wants to buy a computer that costs $1,500. She has saved $925. How much more does she need? _____

   a. $m - 925 = 1{,}500$ **b.** $m + 925 = 1{,}500$ **c.** $925m = 1{,}500$

35. A carpenter will cut 6 shelves of equal length from a 96-inch-long board. How long will each shelf be? _____

   a. $\frac{e}{6} = 96$ **b.** $6e = 96$ **c.** $e + 6 = 96$

36. An oil tank truck made deliveries of 1,575 gallons of oil in a single day. At the end of the day, there were 30 gallons of oil left in the truck. How many gallons did the truck start with? _____

   a. $30g = 1{,}575$ **b.** $g + 1{,}575 = 30$ **c.** $g - 1{,}575 = 30$

Apply the Idea

37. An electrical supply company has 174 feet of cable that can be used to make extension cords. Write and solve an equation to find how many 6-foot extension cords can be cut from the cable. Let x stand for the number of 6-foot extension cords that can be cut from the cable.

_____

Write About It

38. a. Tell what you would do first to solve this equation.
    $3(x + 2) = 18$

_____

   b. What other first step could you take to solve the equation?

_____

Chapter 2   Review

In This Chapter, You Have Learned
- To recognize equations and their solutions
- To solve equations using addition and subtraction
- To solve equations using multiplication and division

Words You Know

From the lists of "Words to Learn," choose the word or phrase that names each definition.

1. A statement that two expressions are equal _____

2. The value of the variable that makes an equation true _____

3. Operations that are opposite _____

4. A rule stating that if you multiply each side of an equation by the same number, the sides are still equal _____

More Practice

Write the letter, a, b, or c, to show the solution to the equation.

5. $w + 12 = 31$ **a.** $w = 12$ **b.** $w = 19$ **c.** $w = 43$ _____

6. $x - 14 = 10$ **a.** $x = 4$ **b.** $x = 10$ **c.** $x = 24$ _____

7. $5y = 35$ **a.** $y = 5$ **b.** $y = 7$ **c.** $y = 30$ _____

8. $\frac{z}{6} = 30$ **a.** $z = 5$ **b.** $z = 24$ **c.** $z = 180$ _____

Solve each equation.

9. $a + 4 = 7$

10. $d - 6 = 2$

11. $e - 24 = 76$

12. $f - 35 = 68$

13. $9d = 27$

14. $d + 21 = 34$

15. $\frac{c}{3} = 24$

16. $4b = 32$

17. $f + 29 = 50$

18. $7a = 63$

19. $\frac{b}{4} = 12$

20. $\frac{d}{6} = 36$

Problems You Can Solve

21. Sam and Leon want to buy a used car. They save the same amount of money and Sam borrows another $400 to put toward the car. They buy a car that costs $1,100. How much money had Sam saved for the car before he borrowed the $400? _____

22. It took Sam and Leon 6 months to save enough money for their car. How much could they have afforded if they had saved at the same rate for another year? _____

23. If they save for another 6 months, and each one borrows $300, how much can they spend for a car? _____

24. **For Your Portfolio** You have a gift certificate for $100 from a mail-order catalogue to spend on clothes. Decide which of the items below you would like to buy and how many of each you want. Write an order to the company that will be close to $100. The total must include a shipping-and-handling charge of $4.

Flannel shirt – $24	Jeans – $36
Pair of socks – $2	T-shirt – $12

ORDER FORM

Customer Fill Out:

Name _____

Address _____

_____

Item	Price per Item	Quantity	Totals
_____	$ _____	_____	$ _____
_____	$ _____	_____	$ _____
_____	$ _____	_____	$ _____
_____	$ _____	_____	$ _____
_____	$ _____	_____	$ _____

Shipping and Handling Charge: $ _____

Total Charge: $ _____

Chapter 2   Practice Test

Write the letter, *a*, *b*, or *c*, that shows the solution to the equation.

1. $x + 11 = 19$ **a.** $x = 8$ **b.** $x = 11$ **c.** $x = 30$ _____
2. $y - 15 = 21$ **a.** $y = 6$ **b.** $y = 15$ **c.** $y = 36$ _____
3. $4w = 36$ **a.** $w = 4$ **b.** $w = 9$ **c.** $w = 32$ _____
4. $\frac{z}{6} = 24$ **a.** $z = 4$ **b.** $z = 30$ **c.** $z = 144$ _____

Solve each equation.

5. $x - 7 = 126$ 6. $y + 18 = 45$

7. $y - 55 = 62$ 8. $x + 22 = 41$

9. $x + 4 = 18$ 10. $y + 9 = 21$

11. $7e = 147$ 12. $e + 53 = 73$

13. $3c = 75$ 14. $f + 25 = 81$

15. $\frac{f}{24} = 30$ 16. $4b = 88$

17. $\frac{b}{4} = 6$ 18. $5d = 95$

Solve.

19. On June 1, half of a company's employees went to a training class. On June 2, three new employees joined the class. Then, there were 35 people in the class. How many company employees were there on June 1? _____

20. If the company's goal is to train $\frac{3}{4}$ of their employees with the new class, how many more must be trained on June 1?

_____

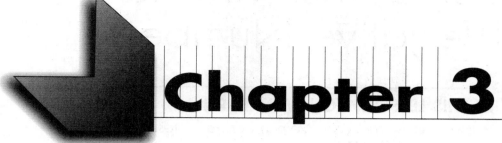

Chapter 3

Positive and Negative Numbers

OBJECTIVES:

In this chapter, you will learn

- *To add, subtract, multiply, and divide positive and negative numbers*
- *To solve one-step equations involving positive and negative numbers*

How cold you feel when you are outdoors depends not only on the air temperature but also on the speed of the wind. In winter, when you listen to a weather report, you may hear the wind speed reported as the *wind-chill temperature.*

The table at right is one example of the way positive and negative numbers are used. It shows wind-chill temperatures for several different combinations of air temperature and wind speed. You can tell from the table, for example, that when the temperature outside is 10°F and the wind speed is 15 miles per hour, the wind-chill temperature is −18°.

Wind-Chill Temperatures

Wind Speed (mi/h)	Air Temperature (°F)								
	30	25	20	15	10	5	0	−5	−10
5	27	21	19	12	7	0	−5	−10	−15
10	16	10	3	−3	−9	−15	−22	−27	−34
15	9	2	−5	−11	−18	−25	−31	−38	−45
20	4	3	−10	−17	−24	−31	−39	−46	−53

◄3•1 Using Positive and Negative Numbers

◄ IN THIS LESSON, YOU WILL LEARN

To use positive and negative numbers to represent real-life situations

WORDS TO LEARN

Positive number *a number that is greater than 0*
Negative number *a number that is less than 0*

A hot-air balloonist launches her balloon. Within a few minutes, she is drifting at a height of 250 meters above the sea level. Later, she is flying over the Dead Sea (the lowest body of water on earth). She loses altitude and descends to a level 40 meters below sea level. How can the balloonist use numbers to express the different heights of the balloon?

New Idea

A number whose value is greater than zero is a **positive number** (PAHZ-uh-tihv NUM-buhr). A number whose value is less than zero is a **negative number** (NEHG-uh-tihv NUM-buhr). All of the numbers you have been using so far in this book are positive numbers.

In the story above, think of sea level as the zero point. At first, the balloonist is 250 meters *above* sea level. We can express this as +250. When flying over the Dead Sea, she is 40 meters *below* sea level. We can express this as −40. The number +250 may also be written without a positive sign as 250. It is read as "positive 250." The number −40 is read as "negative 40."

◄ Focus on the Idea

Positive numbers have values greater than 0.
Negative numbers have values less than 0.

Practice

Write a positive number or negative number for each situation.

1. loss of 25 lb _____

2. increase of 50 votes _____

3. gaining 40 yd _____

4. 65° above zero _____

5. losing 25 yd

_____

6. 12° below zero

_____

7. 12,000 ft above sea level

_____

8. 450 ft below sea level

_____

9. 12 steps backward

_____

10. 5° below zero

_____

11. 25 m below sea level

_____

12. gaining 2 points

_____

13. 15 steps forward

_____

14. gain of 2 kg

_____

15. 15 ft above ground

_____

16. receiving 3 presents

_____

17. use of 14 gal of gas

_____

18. 5 cm below ground

_____

Apply the Idea

19. Jake is a stamp collector who buys and sells stamps. Last week, Jake completed these transactions: bought 2 stamps; sold 4 stamps; sold 1 stamp; bought 12 stamps; sold 7 stamps. Describe each transaction, using positive and negative numbers.

a. bought 2 stamps _____

b. sold 4 stamps _____

c. sold 1 stamp _____

d. bought 12 stamps _____

e. sold 7 stamps _____

Write About It

20. Explain how negative numbers can be used to represent other real-life situations. Give some examples.

_____

_____

_____

►3•2 Using a Number Line

The low temperature in Anchorage one day was $-11°$F. In Fairbanks, the low temperature was $-20°$F. Which temperature was lower?

New Idea

A **number line** (NUM-buhr lyen) is a diagram on which positive numbers, negative numbers, and zero can be located. On a horizontal number line, positive numbers appear to the right of zero. Negative numbers appear to the left of zero. The arrows on either end of the number line indicate that the numbers continue in both directions.

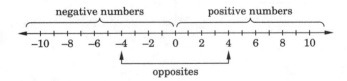

On the number line, the numbers -4 and 4 are each 4 units from 0, but in opposite directions. They are called **opposite numbers** (AHP-uh-ziht NUM-buhrz).

Since numbers increase in value, from left to right, along a number line, **inequality symbols** (ihn-ee-KWAHL-uh-tee SIHM-buhlz) are used to compare two numbers. The symbol " $<$ " means "is less than." The symbol " $>$ " means "is greater than."

Examples: Compare 1 and -4. Use the number line to help.

Locate 1 and -4 on the number line above. Since 1 is farther to the right, 1 is greater than -4, or $1 > -4$.

Now you can answer the question at the beginning of the lesson. The temperature in Fairbanks was lower than the temperature in Anchorage, because −20 is to the left of −11 on the number line.

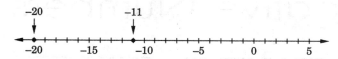

Focus on the Idea

A number line can be used to show positive numbers, negative numbers, and zero. Numbers increase in value from left to right. Opposite numbers are the same distance from zero, but in different directions.

Practice

Compare. Write < or >. The first one is done for you.

1. 2 _____>_____ −5　　**2.** −5 _____ −7　　**3.** −8 _____ 6

4. 12 _____ −1　　**5.** −7 _____ −5　　**6.** −6 _____ 3

Write the number that is at each lettered point on the number line.

7. A ____　**8.** E ____　**9.** C ____　**10.** F ____　**11.** B ____　**12.** D ____

Write the opposite of each number.

13. −4 _____　　**14.** 1 _____　　**15.** −11 _____

Apply the Idea

The thermometer shows high temperatures for several cities on one day.

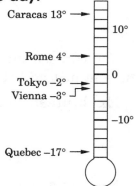

16. Which city had the coldest temperature? _____

17. Which city had the warmer temperature, Tokyo or Vienna? _____

18. Are the colder temperatures near the top or near the bottom? _____

✎ Write About It

19. Explain how to compare negative numbers. Give an example.

_____

_____

Adding Positive and Negative Numbers

To add positive and negative numbers

WORDS TO LEARN
Unit *a single quantity of measurement*

At 6:00 o'clock in the morning, the temperature was $-7°F$. By noon, the temperature had risen $10°$. What was the temperature at noon?

New Idea

A horizontal number line can be used to help you add two positive numbers or two negative numbers. Each space on the number line represents one **unit** (YOO-niht) or a single quantity of measurement.

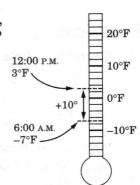

Examples: Use the number line to add these integers.

To add $4 + 5$, begin at zero. Move to 4 on the number line. Then move 5 units to the right.

To add $-3 + (-5)$, begin at zero. Move to -3 on the number line. Then move -5 units, or 5 units to the left.

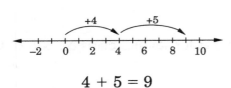

$$4 + 5 = 9$$

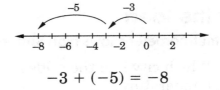

$$-3 + (-5) = -8$$

You can see that when adding two numbers that have the same sign, you just add the numbers and write their sign in the sum.

Examples: Find the sums. $-7 + (-9)$ $11 + 2$

$$-7 + (-9) = -16$$

$$11 + 2 = 13$$

You can also use a number line to help you add two numbers with different signs—a positive number and a negative number.

Examples: Use the number line to add.

To add $2 + (-10)$, begin at zero and move to 2. Then move -10 units, or 10 units to the left.

To add $-6 + 8$, begin at zero. Move to -6. Then move 8 units to the right.

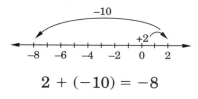

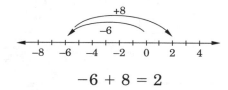

$$2 + (-10) = -8$$

$$-6 + 8 = 2$$

When adding two numbers that have different signs first subtract the numbers, then write the sign of the number farthest from zero.

Examples: Add. $-15 + 44$

First subtract the numbers: $44 - 15 = 29$. Then decide which number is farthest from zero. Write the sign of 44, since it is farther from zero than -15. (The sign of 44 is positive.) The answer, 29, is positive: $-15 + 44 = 29$.

Look back at the question about noon temperature.

The temperature at 6:00 o'clock in the morning was $-7°$. By noon it had increased $10°$. To find the temperature at noon, find the sum, $-7 + 10$.

Since the signs of the numbers are different, first subtract the numbers: $10 - 7 = 3$. Since 10 is farther from zero than -7, write the sign of the 10, which is positive: $-7 + 10 = 3$. The temperature at noon was $3°F$.

✓ **Check the Math**

1. Antoine added a negative number and a positive number. He wrote, $-11 + 20 = -31$. Is he correct? _____

◢ **Focus on the Idea**

Follow these rules when adding positive and negative numbers:
- *If the numbers have the same signs, add them and write their sign in the sum.*
- *If the numbers have different signs, first subtract one from the other; then write the sign of the number farthest from zero in the sum.*

Practice

Write an addition sentence for each number line. The first one is done for you.

2.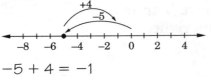

$$-5 + 4 = -1$$

3.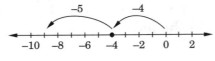

_____

4.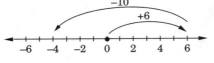

_____

5.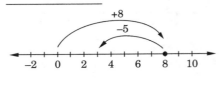

_____

Mark and label a number line to help you find each sum.

6. $-3 + 6 = $ _____

7. $-5 + 1 = $ _____

8. $-3 + (-2) = $ _____

9. $2 + 1 = $ _____

10. $-4 + 9 = $ _____

11. $-6 + 7 = $ _____

12. $-8 + 3 = $ _____

13. $-1 + (-7) = $ _____

Extend the Idea

When there are three or more numbers to be added with different signs, it is often a good idea to add those with like signs first, then subtract. Write the sign of the number farthest from zero on the number line.

Example: Add 12, −7, 9, and −10.

First add 12 and 9, then −7 and −10. $12 + 9 = 21$; $-7 + -10 = -17$. Now subtract 21 and 17. Because 21 is farther from zero on the number line than −17, the sign will be positive. $21 + (-17) = 4$

✓Check Your Understanding

14. Give an example of an addition problem with positive and negative numbers that results in a positive sum.

_____

Practice

Write an addition sentence for each number line. The first one is done for you.

15.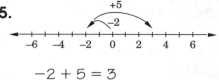

$$-2 + 5 = 3$$

16.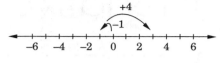

_____

17.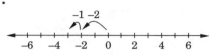

_____

18.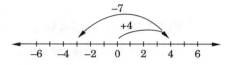

_____

Add.

19. $-3 + (-5) =$ _____

20. $-1 + 2 =$ _____

21. $-4 + 7 =$ _____

22. $9 + (-3) =$ _____

23. $2 + (-5) =$ _____

24. $-1 + (-3) =$ _____

25. $-2 + (-5) =$ _____

26. $-8 + 1 =$ _____

27. $-3 + (-9) + 5 + (-2) =$ _____

28. $-7 + (-2) + 5 =$ _____

29. $10 + (-1) + (-4) =$ _____

30. $-12 + 3 + 1 + (-8) =$ _____

Apply the Idea

31. Part of the city of New Orleans is 4 feet below sea level. Another part of the city is 19 feet higher. How far above sea level is the higher point of the city? _____

32. When Mario left for work in the morning, the temperature was $-1°C$. By the time he arrived home in the evening, the temperature had risen $5°C$. What was the evening temperature? _____

Write About It

33. You have learned that positive numbers can be added in any order and their sum will be the same. So, $2 + 5 = 7$ and $5 + 2 = 7$. Can negative numbers also be added in any order? Use examples to explain your answer.

_____

_____

◢3•4 Subtracting Positive and Negative Numbers

◥ IN THIS LESSON, YOU WILL LEARN
To subtract positive and negative numbers

WORDS TO LEARN
Elevation *the height of an object or place*

The height or **elevation** (eh-luh-VAY-shuhn) of the lowest point of the Sahara Desert in Africa is −440 feet (440 feet below sea level). The elevation of the Nubian Desert in Africa is 2,500 feet. What is the difference in elevation between these two points?

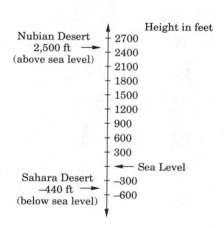

New Idea

You can use a number line to subtract positive and negative numbers. First, locate each number on the line. Then, find the distance from the second number to the first number. On a horizontal number line, if you are moving to the right to get to the first number, the sign of the difference is positive. If you are moving to the left to get to the first number, the sign of the difference is negative.

Examples: Find the difference. Use the number line to help you.

Subtract 2 from −3.

Draw an arrow from 2, five units to get to −3.

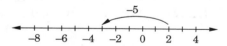

The difference: $-3 - 2 = -5$

Subtract −6 from 4.

Draw an arrow from −6, ten units to get to 4.

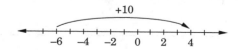

The difference: $4 - (-6) = 10$

1. How can you use the number line to subtract a number from itself? Explain by using a number line to subtract $5 - 5$.

_____

◢ Focus on the Idea

To find the difference between two numbers on a number line, first locate each number. Then find the distance from the second number to the first. If you are moving to the right as you do this, the sign of the difference is positive. If you are moving to the left, the sign of the difference is negative.

Practice

Complete the subtraction sentence for each number line diagram. The first one is done for you.

2.

$-3 - (-4) =$ _____1_____

3.
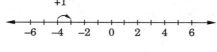

$2 - 5 =$ _____

4.
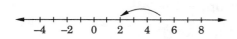

$-5 - 1 =$ _____

Mark and label a number line to help you find each difference.

5. $-5 - 4 =$ _____

6. $2 - 10 =$ _____

7. $-3 - (-1) =$ _____

8. $7 - (-3) =$ _____

9. $8 - 6 =$ _____

10. $12 - 12 =$ _____

Mark and label a number line for each pair of subtraction and addition exercises.

11. **a.** $5 - 2 =$ _____   ←——+—+—+—+—+—+—+—+—+—+—+→

      b. $5 + (-2) =$ _____   ←——+—+—+—+—+—+—+—+—+—+—→

12. **a.** $-4 - (-2) =$ _____   ←——+—+—+—+—+—+—+—+—+—+→

      b. $-4 + 2 =$ _____   ←——+—+—+—+—+—+—+—+—+—+→

13. **a.** $3 - (-2) =$ _____   ←——+—+—+—+—+—+—+—+—+—+→

      b. $3 + 2 =$ _____   ←——+—+—+—+—+—+—+—+—+—+→

14. **a.** $-3 - (-7) =$ _____   ←——+—+—+—+—+—+—+—+—+—+→

      b. $-3 + 7 =$ _____   ←——+—+—+—+—+—+—+—+—+—+→

Extend the Idea

Subtracting a number is the same as adding the opposite of that number. First, find the opposite of the number being subtracted. Then use the rules for adding positive and negative numbers.

Examples: Subtract. $-4 - (-2)$

Think: the opposite of -2 is 2.

Rewrite $-4 - (-2)$ as an addition, $-4 + 2$.

Since the signs are different, think of $4 - 2 = 2$.

Since -4 is farther from 0, the difference is negative.

$$-4 - (-2) = -4 + 2$$
$$= -2$$

Subtract. $-10 - 8$

Think: the opposite of 8 is -8.

Rewrite $-10 - 8$ as an addition, $-10 + (-8)$.

Since the signs are the same, add and use the negative sign.

$$-10 - 8 = -10 + (-8)$$
$$= -18$$

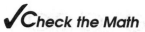

15. Raoul said that sometimes the difference between two negative numbers is a positive number. Is he right? Give an example to support your answer.

_____

Practice

Subtract. First, rewrite each subtraction sentence as an addition sentence. The first one is done for you.

16. $-2 - (-6) = -2 +$ ____6____ $=$ ____4____

17. $-7 - (-5) = -7 +$ _____ $=$ _____

18. $6 - 8 = 6 +$ _____ $=$ _____

19. $-4 - (-1) = -4 +$ _____ $=$ _____

Find each difference.

20. $6 - 11 =$ _____   **21.** $-3 - 8 =$ _____

22. $-7 - (-2) =$ _____   **23.** $1 - (-7) =$ _____

24. $-6 - 8 =$ _____   **25.** $-9 - (-1) =$ _____

Apply the Idea

26. At 7:30 A.M., the temperature was $-4°C$. By 1:30 P.M., the temperature was $10°C$. Circle the phrase that describes the change in temperature.

  a. increased by $14°$

  b. decreased by $14°$

  c. increased by $6°$

Write About It

27. Imagine you are a sixth-grade math teacher. You are teaching your students about adding and subtracting integers. You have made a walk-on number line. Explain how you would use it with your class.

_____

_____

_____

3•5 Multiplying Positive and Negative Numbers

IN THIS LESSON, YOU WILL LEARN
To multiply positive and negative numbers

WORDS TO LEARN
Deduct *to take away or subtract from*
Deposit *to put in or add to*

Eleanor will **deduct** (dee-DUHKT), or take away, $25 from her checking account every week and will **deposit** (dee-PAW-ziht), or add, it to her savings account. How much money will be deducted from her checking account after 7 weeks?

New Idea
One way to look at multiplication, such as (3)(4), is as repeated addition:

$$(3)(4) = 4 + 4 + 4 \qquad \leftarrow 3 \text{ fours are added.}$$

This idea helps us find a product like 3 times −4:

$$(3)(-4) = -4 + -4 + -4 \quad \leftarrow 3 \text{ negative fours are added.}$$
$$= -12$$

Therefore, $(3)(-4) = -12$.

Remember
The commutative property of multiplication states that you can change the order of numbers when you multiply. So, for example, since $(3)(-4) = -12$, the commutative property tells us that $(-4)(3) = -12$.

Here is a rule for multiplying positive and negative numbers:
When two numbers have different signs, their product is negative. For example, $(4)(-7) = -28$ and $(-6)(8) = -48$.

Example: To find the amount of money to be deducted from Eleanor's checking account, multiply −25 times 7.

$$(-25)(7) = -175$$

So, the checking account will be decreased by $175 after 7 weeks.

You know that when two positive numbers are multiplied, their product is positive. To see what happens when two negative numbers are multiplied, look at this pattern for multiplying numbers by -3.

$$(-3)(3) = -9$$
$$(-3)(2) = -6$$
$$(-3)(1) = -3$$
$$(-3)(0) = 0$$

How would you describe the pattern?

The next sentences in this pattern should be:

$$(-3)(-1) = 3$$
$$(-3)(-2) = 6$$
$$(-3)(-3) = 9$$

The pattern shows that if two negative numbers are multiplied, their product is positive.

Focus on the Idea

The product of two numbers with different signs is negative. The product of two numbers with the same signs is positive.

Practice

Multiply. The first two are done for you.

1. $(-2)(5) = \underline{\quad -10 \quad}$ 2. $(-4)(-8) = \underline{\quad 32 \quad}$ 3. $(-3)(9) = \underline{\qquad}$

4. $(8)(-3) = \underline{\qquad}$ 5. $(3)(-7) = \underline{\qquad}$ 6. $(5)(3) = \underline{\qquad}$

7. $(-2)(8) = \underline{\qquad}$ 8. $(-1)(-9) = \underline{\qquad}$ 9. $(9)(-5) = \underline{\qquad}$

10. $(7)(-6) = \underline{\qquad}$ 11. $(-90)(-3) = \underline{\qquad}$ 12. $(-4)(25) = \underline{\qquad}$

Apply the Idea

13. The temperature is dropping at a rate of $2°$ per hour. Find the change in temperature after six hours. _____

14. Felix is charged a $5 fee on his checking account each month. Write the change in the amount in his checking account after seven months. _____

Write About It

15. Explain why the product of two negative numbers is positive.

_____

_____

_____

▶3•6 Dividing Positive and Negative Numbers

▶ IN THIS LESSON, YOU WILL LEARN

To divide positive and negative numbers

WORDS TO LEARN

Related sentences *number sentences that involve inverse operations*

At noon, the outdoor temperature was 70°F. By 3:00 P.M. the wind had shifted and the temperature dropped to 58°F. What was the rate of temperature change per hour?

New Idea

A multiplication sentence and a division sentence are **related sentences** (rih-LAYT-ihd SEHN-tuhn-suhz) when they involve inverse operations.

$2 \cdot 10 = 20$ is related to: $20 \div 10 = 2$ and $20 \div 2 = 10$

To solve a division sentence like $21 \div -7 = ?$, look at the related multiplication sentence:

$? \cdot (-7) = 21$

The answer is -3. Therefore, $21 \div -7$ must be -3.

Examples: Here are some related sentences. Look for patterns.

$$32 \div -8 = -4 \text{ since } (-8)(-4) = 32$$

$$-18 \div 2 = -9 \text{ since } (2)(-9) = -18$$

$$-48 \div -6 = 8 \text{ since } (-6)(8) = -48$$

Compare the signs in each pair of division and multiplication examples. The rule for dividing positive and negative numbers is the same as the rule for multiplying them. If the numbers being divided have the same sign, the quotient is positive. If the numbers being divided have different signs, the quotient is negative.

Example: Find the rate of temperature change per hour.

The difference between the 3:00 P.M. and noon temperatures is $58 - 70 = -12$. The rate of change is found by dividing -12 by 3. The result is -4. The temperature changed by $-4°$ per hour, which means it decreased by 4° each hour.

Focus on the Idea

The quotient of two numbers with different signs is negative. The quotient of two numbers with the same signs is positive.

Practice

Complete each division sentence. Then write it as a related multiplication sentence. The first one is done for you.

Division sentence   *Multiplication sentence*

1. $-24 \div 8 = $ _____-3_____ $8 \cdot$ _____-3_____ $= -24$

2. $15 \div -5 = $ _____ $-5 \cdot$ _____ $= 15$

3. $-72 \div -9 = $ _____ $-9 \cdot$ _____ $= -72$

Find each quotient.

4. $-81 \div -9 = $ _____   5. $-54 \div 9 = $ _____

6. $60 \div -10 = $ _____   7. $-75 \div -5 = $ _____

8. $100 \div -4 = $ _____   9. $-350 \div 7 = $ _____

10. $-381 \div -3 = $ _____   11. $564 \div -4 = $ _____

12. $-44 \div 11 = $ _____   13. $600 \div -3 = $ _____

14. $-507 \div -3 = $ _____   15. $-144 \div -12 = $ _____

Apply the Idea

16. The temperature dropped from 12°F to −8°F in five hours.

    a. By how much did the temperature change? _____

    b. What was the temperature change per hour? _____

    c. Predict the temperature in two more hours. _____

Write About It

17. If a times b equals c, explain why you can be sure that c divided by b equals a. Substitute numbers for these variables and use them to make up an example to prove this point. Show that the rule is true for negative and positive numbers.

    _____

    _____

3•7 Solving Equations Using Positive and Negative Numbers

IN THIS LESSON, YOU WILL LEARN

To solve one-step equations involving positive and negative numbers

WORDS TO LEARN

One-step equation *an equation that can be solved in a single operation*

A chemist heated a liquid 50° to a temperature of 38°F. What was the temperature of the liquid before it was heated?

New Idea

You can write a one-step equation for many problems and then solve it using the rules for positive and negative numbers. A **one-step equation** (wuhn-stehp ee-KWAY-zhuhn) is one that can be solved in a single operation. Use the same steps you used to solve equations with only positive numbers.

Examples: Solve the chemist's problem. Write an equation where x is the temperature of the liquid before it was heated.

$$x + 50 = 38$$
$$x + 50 - 50 = 38 - 50 \quad \leftarrow \text{Subtract 50 from both sides.}$$
$$x = 38 + -50 \leftarrow \text{Subtract by adding the opposite.}$$
$$x = -12$$

The temperature of the liquid was $-12°$F.

$$2x = -146 \quad \leftarrow \text{If } x \text{ is multiplied by 2, the result is } -146.$$
$$\frac{2x}{2} = \frac{-146}{2} \quad \leftarrow \text{Divide each side by 2.}$$
$$x = -73 \quad \leftarrow \text{The solution is } -73.$$

Focus on the Idea

The rules for solving equations with positive and negative numbers are exactly the same as the rules for solving equations with positive numbers.

Practice

Complete each equation to find the solution. The first one is done for you.

1. $x + 21 = 4$
    $x + 21 - 21 = 4 - 21$
    $x = -17$

2. $x + 7 = -3$

    $x =$ _____

3. $-5x = -100$

    $x =$ _____

4. $3x = -48$

    $x =$ _____

Solve each equation.

5. $x + 9 = 3$ _____

6. $x + 5 = -11$ _____

7. $x - 2 = -12$ _____

8. $x - 7 = -1$ _____

9. $4x = -28$ _____

10. $-3x = -27$ _____

11. $\frac{x}{-3} = 8$ _____

12. $\frac{x}{4} = -5$ _____

Apply the Idea

Choose an equation for the problem. Then solve that equation.

13. The temperature changed by 8° in the last 2 hours. By how many degrees per hour did the temperature change?

    a. $-8x = 2$ **b.** $2x = 8$ **c.** $x + 2 = -8$

    _____

14. A race car decreased its speed by 12 miles per hour, to 92 miles per hour. What was its original speed?

    a. $x + 12 = 92$ **b.** $12x = 92$ **c.** $x - 12 = 92$

    _____

Write About It

15. Write a paragraph to explain the solution of $4x = -24$.

    _____

    _____

    _____

Chapter 3   Review

In This Chapter, You Have Learned

- To use positive and negative numbers in real-life situations
- To locate positive and negative numbers on a number line
- To find opposite numbers
- To compare positive and negative numbers, using the inequality symbols, $<$ and $>$
- To add, subtract, multiply, and divide positive and negative numbers
- To solve one-step equations involving positive and negative numbers

Words You Know

From the lists of "Words to Learn," choose the word or phrase that best completes each statement.

1. The symbols $<$ and $>$ are called _____.

2. A(n) _____ is a number less than zero.

3. A(n) _____ is a number greater than zero.

More Practice

Write a positive or a negative number for each situation.

4. 3,000 feet below sea level   5. 6° above zero

_____   _____

6. A gain of 50 yards   7. An increase of 97

_____   _____

Write the number that is below each letter on the number line.

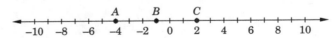

8. A _____   9. C _____   10. B _____

Write the opposite of each number.

11. 2 _____   12. 5 _____   13. -15 _____

Compare each pair of numbers using $<$ or $>$.

14. -2 _____ -3 15. -1 _____ -5 16. -6 _____ -5

Solve.

17. $-3 + (-8) =$ _____
18. $6 + (-9) =$ _____

19. $-2 + 8 =$ _____
20. $10 + (-3) =$ _____

21. $6 - 10 =$ _____
22. $-3 - 8 =$ _____

23. $-7 - (-2) =$ _____
24. $13 - (-1) =$ _____

25. $(5)(-5) =$ _____
26. $(-7)(4) =$ _____

27. $(-4)(-11) =$ _____
28. $(10)(-30) =$ _____

29. $-49 \div 7 =$ _____
30. $-36 \div -4 =$ _____

31. $100 \div -20 =$ _____
32. $60 \div -15 =$ _____

Solve each equation.

33. $x - 14 = -30$ _____
34. $x + 5 = -21$ _____

35. $-3x = 18$ _____
36. $\frac{x}{5} = -6$ _____

Problems You Can Solve

37. At 4:00 P.M. the temperature was 4°F. Then it dropped at a rate of 2° per hour. At that rate, what will be the temperature at 9:00 P.M.? _____

38. A submarine went down 22 feet in the water. Then it went up 35 feet. How much higher or lower was the final position of the submarine compared with its original position in the water? _____

39. **For Your Portfolio** Make up a game to play with these two spinners. Describe your game, tell how a player wins, and give an example of a round of play.

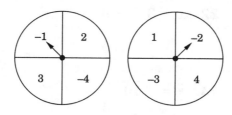

_____

_____

_____

_____

Chapter 3 Practice Test

Write a positive or a negative number for each situation.

1. 5,000 feet above sea level

   _____

2. 8° below zero

   _____

3. A loss of 25 yd

   _____

4. A credit of $50

   _____

Write the number at each lettered point on the number line.

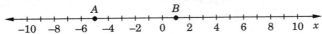

5. A _____

6. B _____

Write the opposite of each number.

7. -7 _____

8. 25 _____

Compare. Write $<$ or $>$.

9. -1 _____ -3

10. -8 _____ -5

Solve.

11. $-2 + (-5) =$ _____

12. $6 + (-4) =$ _____

13. $-9 + 8 =$ _____

14. $10 - (-3) =$ _____

15. $-5 - 7 =$ _____

16. $(-7)(-9) =$ _____

17. $4(-10) =$ _____

18. $33 \div -3 =$ _____

19. $-56 \div 7 =$ _____

20. $-36 \div -6 =$ _____

Solve each equation.

21. $x - 1 = -3$

22. $x + 3 = -9$

23. $4x = -28$

24. $\frac{x}{2} = -10$

Solve.

25. Fred's checking account had a balance of $410 on February 1. His check register shows the following: Feb. 2: $35; Feb. 3: -$60; and Feb. 4: -$25. What is his new balance?

    _____

Chapter 4
Factors and Fractions

OBJECTIVES:

In this chapter, you will learn

- *To evaluate a numerical or variable expression*
- *To identify prime and composite numbers*
- *To find the prime factors of a number*
- *To identify monomials and their coefficients*
- *To identify numerical and variable factors of monomials*
- *To identify binomials, trinomials, polynomials, and constant terms*
- *To simplify polynomials by combining like terms*
- *To find the greatest common factor*
- *To write a fraction to describe part of a whole*
- *To identify equivalent fractions*
- *To write a fraction in lowest terms*
- *To find multiples of a number*
- *To find the least common multiple*
- *To compare fractions*

Pages of a book are printed on both sides of large sheets of paper. Each side of a large sheet actually contains 16 pages of the book. So, there are 32 pages per sheet. These large sheets are then folded, cut, and gathered to form a batch.

You can see why multiples and factors of 16 and 32 are very important in the publishing business. Look at your textbooks. How can you find out if the numbers of pages are multiples of 16?

side 1

1	16	13	4
8	9	12	5
17	32	29	20
24	25	28	21

side 2

3	14	15	2
6	11	10	7
19	30	31	18
22	27	26	23

◢4•1 Evaluating Expressions with Exponents

An entrance hall measures 6 feet by 6 feet. A tile mason needs to cover the floor with square tiles that measure 1 foot on a side. How many tiles will be needed?

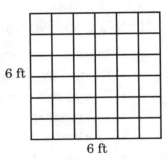

6 ft

6 ft

New Idea

From this diagram of the entrance hall, you can see that the floor is square. All four sides of a square have the same measure. So, to find the area of a square region, multiply the length of one side by itself.

To multiply a number by itself, you can write the product using a **base** (bays) and an **exponent** (EHKS-pohn-uhnt):

$$6 \cdot 6 = 6^2 \leftarrow \text{exponent}$$
$$\uparrow \underline{\hspace{1cm}} \text{base}$$
$$= 36 \leftarrow \text{product}$$

Another way to describe 6^2, is "6 is used as a factor 2 times."

A **factor** (FAK-tuhr) is a number that is multiplied by another number to produce a product.

Examples: Simplify 2^5 and 8^1. For each, name the base, the exponent, and the product.

$$2^5 = 2 \cdot 2 \cdot 2 \cdot 2 \cdot 2 \quad \leftarrow \text{The base is 2, the}$$
$$\text{exponent is 5, and}$$
$$\text{the product is 32.}$$
$$= 32$$

$$8^1 = 8 \cdot 1 \quad \leftarrow \text{The base is 8, the exponent is 1.}$$
$$\text{8 is used as a factor 1 time.}$$

$$= 8$$

1. Name the base, exponent, and product for each statement. The first one is done for you.

Statement	Base	Exponent	Product
$3^4 = 81$	3	4	81
$5^2 = 25$			
$7^3 = 343$			

↩**Remember**

According to the order of operations: 1) work inside parentheses; 2) do all calculations involving exponents if they are present; 3) multiply or divide; and 4) add or subtract.

◤ ## Focus on the Idea

An exponent tells how many times the base is used as a factor. To find the product, multiply the base by itself the number of times indicated by the exponent.

Practice

Find each product. The first one is done for you.

2. $(-7)^2 = \underline{(-7)\,(-7) = 49}$ **3.** $3^3 = $ _____

4. $(-2)^4 = $ _____ **5.** $4^2 = $ _____

6. $(-1)^6 = $ _____ **7.** $(-1)^7 = $ _____

8. $5^3 = $ _____ **9.** $(-4)^3 = $ _____

Simplify each expression, using the order of operations. The first one is done for you.

10. $5 + 3^3 = $
$\underline{5 + 27 = 32}$

11. $8^2 - 4(5) = $ _____

12. $12 \div (-3) + (-2)^3 = $ _____

13. $6^2 - 50 = $ _____

14. $2 - 4^2 = $ _____

15. $9^2 - 3^3 = $ _____

16. $2^4 - 5^2 = $ _____

17. $5 + 10 - 6^2 = $ _____

Extend the Idea

You can evaluate a variable expression, such as $4 + x^3$, by replacing the variable with a number.

Examples: Simplify $4 + x^3$ when $x = -1$.

$$4 + (-1)^3 = 4 + (-1)(-1)(-1)$$

$$= 4 + (-1)$$

$$= 3$$

When $x = -1$, $4 + x^3 = 3$.

In an expression such as $2x^3$, each time you replace x with a different value, $2x^3$ will have a different value. The table shows how $2x^3$ is simplified when $x = -1$, $x = 0$, and $x = 2$.

x	$2x^3$
-1	$(2)(-1)^3 = -2$
0	$(2)(0)^3 = 0$
2	$(2)(2)^3 = 16$

✓Check the Math

18. Kiko said that before simplifying an expression, she could tell the sign of the product. She said that the product $2x^3$ was positive when $x = 2$ and negative when $x = -2$. Was Kiko right? Why?

_____

Practice

Simplify each expression when $x = -2$. The first one is done for you.

19. $x^3 - 1 = \underline{(-2)^3 - 1 = -9}$ 20. $-5x^2 = $ _____

21. $x^3 + 5 = $ _____ 22. $9x^2 = $ _____

Evaluate each expression for the given values of the variable.

23.

x	$-2x^2$
-1	_____
0	_____
2	_____
3	_____

24.

y	$y^4 - 11$
-1	_____
0	_____
1	_____
2	_____

25.

a	$10 - a^2$
-1	_____
0	_____
1	_____
2	_____

26.

g	$8g^3$
-2	_____
-1	_____
0	_____
1	_____

27.

k	$2k + k^2$
-2	_____
-1	_____
0	_____
3	_____

28.

m	$m^3 - m^2$
-2	_____
-1	_____
0	_____
3	_____

Apply the Idea

29. In the wall design shown, black tiles form a 3-foot by 3-foot square within a 9-foot by 9-foot square. The outer tiles are white.

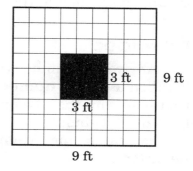

a. Which expression can be used to find the number of 1-foot by 1-foot white tiles that are needed? _____

    A. $9 - 3$ **B.** $9^2 - 3^2$ **C.** $9^3 - 3^2$

b. Find the number of white tiles needed for the wall design. _____

30. An electrician uses the formula $W = I^2R$, where W is the power in watts, I is the current in amperes, and R is the resistance in ohms. Find the power in a household circuit that has 20 amperes of current and 5 ohms of resistance.

_____

✎ Write About It

31. The formula for the volume of a cube is $V = s^3$ where s is the length of one side of the cube. The volume of the cube to the right is $(2 \text{ feet})^3$ or 2 feet • 2 feet • 2 feet. You can read $(2 \text{ feet})^3$ as "2 feet cubed." Explain why $(2 \text{ feet})^2$ is read "2 feet squared." You might draw a diagram to help explain your answer.

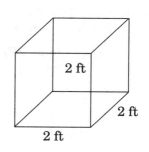

_____

_____

▶4•2 Finding Prime Factors

> ### ▶ IN THIS LESSON, YOU WILL LEARN
> To identify prime and composite numbers
> To find the prime factors of a number
>
> ### WORDS TO LEARN
> **Prime number** *a whole number whose only factors are 1 and the number itself*
> **Composite number** *a whole number that has more than two factors*
> **Prime factorization** *the value of a composite number written as a product of its prime numbers*

Asa has 24 co-workers in his department. They are going to form work groups for a new project. Asa has to decide how many equal groups to set up and the number of people in each.

New Idea

Any whole number whose only factors are 1 and the number itself is called a **prime number** (preyem NUM-buhr). Any whole number that has more than two factors is called a **composite number** (kum-PAHZ-iht NUM-buhr).

You can factor a composite number by writing it as a product of its factors.

Example: Write 24 as a product of its factors.

$$24 = 1 \cdot 24,\ 2 \cdot 12,\ 3 \cdot 8,\text{ or } 4 \cdot 6$$

The factors of 24 are 1, 24, 2, 12, 3, 8, 4 and 6.

Asa can set up 2 groups of 12 people, 12 groups of 2, 3 groups of 8, 8 groups of 3, 4 groups of 6, or 6 groups of 4.

Writing a composite number as a product of its *prime factors* is called the **prime factorization** (preyem fak-tuhr-ih-ZAY-shuhn) of the number. You can make factor trees to find prime factorizations.

Examples: Write the prime factorization for each of 24 and 45 as a product using exponents.

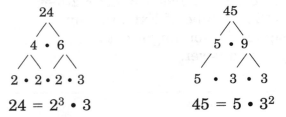

Focus on the Idea

A prime number is a whole number with only two factors, 1 and the number itself. A composite number is a whole number with more than two factors. Any composite number can be written as a product of its prime factors, which is called a prime factorization.

Practice

Write *P* for each prime number and *C* for each composite number.

1. 23 _____   2. 39 _____   3. 91 _____   4. 51 _____

5. 9 _____   6. 99 _____   7. 37 _____   8. 43 _____

Write each number as the product of its prime factors.

9. $26 =$ _____   10. $35 =$ _____   11. $44 =$ _____

12. $18 =$ _____   13. $28 =$ _____   14. $27 =$ _____

Draw a factor tree starting with two factors of the number. Then write the prime factorization using exponents. The first one is done for you.

15. 36   16. 21   17. 8   18. 54

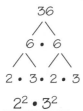

$$\underline{2^2 \cdot 3^2}$$

_____   _____   _____

Apply the Idea

19. Nick has a job at a supermarket. He needs to arrange 48 cans of soup in three equal layers on the shelf. Write each different arrangement as a number of rows and the number of cans in each row.

_____

✎ Write About It

20. The numbers 0 and 1 are neither prime nor composite. Explain why this is true.

_____

_____

▶4•3 Identifying Monomials and Their Factors

▶ **IN THIS LESSON, YOU WILL LEARN**

To identify monomials and their coefficients

To identify numerical and variable factors of monomials

WORDS TO LEARN

Monomial *a number, a variable, or a product of numbers and variables*

Coefficient *the number part of a monomial*

Constant *a monomial with no variables*

Common factors *numbers or variables that are factors of two or more monomials*

Some road crews use plastic water containers shaped like cubes. A cubic foot equals 7.48 gallons. A road crew's water container has a side of x feet. This container can hold $7.48x^3$ gallons. The road crew needs to know how much water they have for the day. By the end of this lesson, you will be able to help them find out.

New Idea

A **monomial** (moh-NOH-mee-uhl) is a number, a variable, or a product of numbers and variables. The number part is called the **coefficient** (kuh-uh-FIHSH-uhnt) of the monomial.

A monomial that is a single number without a variable is called a **constant** (KAHN-stuhnt). A monomial must be a single product and cannot have a variable in a denominator.

Examples: These are monomials. $7, -9y^4, 2\frac{ab}{3}$

These are *not* monomials. $8 + z, 4\frac{ab}{c}, 2y^2 - 3$

7 is the coefficient of $7x^2$.

$\frac{2}{3}$ is the coefficient of $\frac{2ab}{3}$.

1 is the coefficient of x^2y.

If two monomials have the same factors, then those numbers or variables are called **common factors** (KAHM-uhn FAK-tuhrz). To find the common factors for two monomials, factor each monomial by writing it as a product of all its factors.

Examples: Find the common factors for $8y^2$ and $-2y^4$.

Factors of $8y^2$: $\underline{2} \cdot 2 \cdot 2 \cdot \underline{y} \cdot \underline{y}$

Factors of $-2y^4$: $-1 \cdot \underline{2} \cdot \underline{y} \cdot \underline{y} \cdot y \cdot y$

The underlined numbers and variables are common to both monomials. The common factor of $8y^2$ and $-2y^4$ is $2 \cdot y \cdot y$, or $2y^2$.

Focus on the Idea

A monomial is a number, a variable, or a product of numbers and variables. The number part of a monomial is called the coefficient. Two monomials may have common factors.

Practice

Tell if each expression is a monomial. Write *yes* or *no*. The first one is done for you.

1. $4x^2$ _____yes_____

2. $-7y^8$ _____

3. $\frac{4}{x^2}$ _____

4. $\frac{b^2}{2}$ _____

5. $6x$ _____

6. $5 + x^2$ _____

Write the coefficient of each monomial. The first one is done for you.

7. y^3 ___1___

8. $-5x^4$ _____

9. $2ab^5$ _____

10. $-6z$ _____

11. $-c^7$ _____

12. $\frac{-2a}{5}$ _____

13. $-w^3$ _____

14. $\frac{k}{3}$ _____

Write the letter that shows the common factor of the pair of monomials.

15. $7x^2$ and $-2x^2$ **a.** 2   **b.** 7   **c.** x^2 _____

16. $9b^2$ and $6a^3$ **a.** 3   **b.** a **c.** b _____

17. $12a^2$ and $4a^3$ **a.** $4a^3$ **b.** $4a^2$ **c.** $12a^2$ _____

Apply the Idea

18. Look back to the top of page 66. If the road crew's water container is 4 feet on each side, find the value of $7.48x^3$.

_____

Write About It

19. Explain how a factor tree could help you find the common factors of $3a^2b^3$ and $6ab^2$.

_____

▸4•4 Identifying and Simplifying Polynomials

▸IN THIS LESSON, YOU WILL LEARN

To identify binomials, trinomials, polynomials, and constant terms

To simplify polynomials by combining like terms

WORDS TO LEARN

Term *another name for a monomial*

Polynomial *a monomial or the sum or difference of two or more monomials*

Binomial *a polynomial with two terms*

Trinomial *a polynomial with three terms*

Like terms *terms that have the same variable and the same exponent*

Two landscape designers are planning to enclose two rectangular plots of land, *A* and *B*, for a garden. They have not yet decided on the length and width of each enclosure, but they made this diagram. They can use the diagram to write a variable expression for the total area.

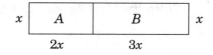

New Idea

A **term** (term) is another name for a monomial. A **polynomial** (pahl-ih-NOH-mee-uhl) is a monomial or the sum or difference of two or more monomials. A polynomial that has two terms is called a **binomial** (by-NOH-mee-uhl). A polynomial that has three terms is called a **trinomial** (try-NOH-mee-uhl). **Like terms** (lyk termz) are terms that have exactly the same variable and the same exponent.

Examples: *Binomial*

$$x + 2y$$

2 terms

Trinomial

$$x^2 - 6x + 1$$

3 terms

Like terms:

$2x$ and $-5x$

$4xy$ and $9xy$

Unlike terms:

$3x$ and $3x^2$

$-8x$ and $7xy$

When a polynomial contains like terms, the like terms can be combined, or simplified. Simplify like terms by adding or subtracting their coefficients.

Examples: Simplify: $-9y^2 + 4y^2 + 3y$

$$-9y^2 + 4y^2 + 3y = -5y^2 + 3y$$

In the landscape designers' diagram, the area for section A is $2x^2$. The area for section B is $3x^2$. The total area is $2x^2 + 3x^2 = 5x^2$.

Focus on the Idea

A polynomial is a sum or difference of monomials. A binomial has two terms and a trinomial has three terms. Polynomials can be simplified by combining their like terms.

Practice

Write the letter of the correct expression.

1. Which expression is a polynomial? _____
   a. -5 **b.** $\frac{8}{x^2}$ **c.** $4x + 8y + z$

2. Which expression is a binomial? _____
   a. $8x + 3$ **b.** $7x^3$ **c.** $2x^2 - 5x - 4$

3. Which expression is a trinomial? _____
   a. $7x + 1$ **b.** $3x + 7y - 2z$ **c.** $9x^3$

Simplify each polynomial, if possible. If the polynomial cannot be simplified, write *not possible*. The first two are done for you.

4. $3x - 2y + 6x$ $\underline{\quad 9x - 2y \quad}$ 5. $8x^2 - 4x - 2$ $\underline{\quad not\ possible \quad}$

6. $9y - 14y$ _____   7. $3x^2 + 5x^2$ _____

8. $4ab - 7b + 2ab$ _____   9. $11y^2 - 3y + 8y^2$ _____

10. $12 - 3ab$ _____   11. $4y + 5x - y$ _____

Apply the Idea

12. A store manager uses x for the number of pounds of spice tea she sells. The tea costs the manager \$2 per pound. She sells it for \$5 per pound. Write a polynomial that expresses her total profit on x pounds of tea. Then simplify it. _____

Write About It

13. A computer spreadsheet is set up with columns and rows. Explain how the store manager mentioned in exercise 12 could use a spreadsheet to calculate her profits. (Hint: Think about how she might label the rows and columns.)

_____

◀4•5 Finding the Greatest Common Factor

Paulo manages a hot dog stand. Hot dog buns are sold in a package of 24. Hot dogs are sold in a package of 36. Paulo wants to store the hot dogs and buns in equal numbers so the servers can make sandwiches quickly. What number of hot dogs and buns should he use?

New Idea

The **greatest common factor** (GRAYT-uhst KAHM-uhn FAK-tuhr) **(GCF)** of two or more numbers is the greatest number that evenly divides all the numbers. You can find the GCF of two numbers by first listing the factors of each.

Example: Find the GCF of 24 and 36.

Factors of 36: 1, 2, 3, 4, 6, 9, 12, 18, and 36
Factors of 24: 1, 2, 3, 4, 6, 8, 12, and 24

The common factors of 36 and 24 are 1, 2, 3, 4, 6, and 12. The greatest of these, the GCF, is 12.

You can also find the GCF of two numbers by first writing the prime factorization of each.

Prime factorization of 36: $2^2 • 3^2$
Prime factorization of 24: $2^3 • 3$
  Common factors of 36 and 24: 2^2 and 3
  Multiply the common factors: $2^2 • 3 = 12$
So, 12 is the GCF of 36 and 24.
This means that Paulo should stack his hot dogs and buns in groups of 12.

Examples: Find the GCF of 10, 15, and 30 by listing the factors.

Factors of 10: 1, 2, 5, 10
Factors of 15: 1, 3, 5, 15
Factors of 30: 1, 2, 3, 5, 6, 10, 15, 30

The common factors of 10, 15, and 30 are 1 and 5. The GCF is 5.

Find the GCF of 10, 15, and 30 by writing the prime factorization.

$$10 = 2 \cdot 5 \qquad 15 = 3 \cdot 5 \qquad 30 = 2 \cdot 3 \cdot 5$$

The only common prime factor of 10, 15, and 30 is 5, so 5 is also the GCF.

Focus on the Idea

The greatest common factor of two or more numbers is the greatest number that divides each of the numbers without a remainder.

Practice

Find the GCF of each set of numbers. The first two are done for you.

1. 8, 10 ___2___
2. 4, 24 ___4___
3. 2, 6 _____
4. 3, 4 _____
5. 3, 12 _____
6. 2, 5 _____
7. 3, 15 _____
8. 4, 10 _____
9. 9, 21 _____
10. 35, 42 _____
11. 12, 20 _____
12. 4, 6, 10 _____
13. 27, 45, 72 _____
14. 20, 45, 50 _____

Apply the Idea

15. Find any two numbers that have a GCF of 6. _____
16. Find any three numbers that have a GCF of 3. _____
17. If two numbers are even, name at least two factors that are common to both. _____

Write About It

18. Tell whether the following statement is true or false. "The GCF of two numbers is always less than either of the numbers." Explain your answer.

_____

_____

◢4•6 Writing Fractions in Lowest Terms

◤ In this lesson, you will learn

To write a fraction to describe part of a whole

To identify equivalent fractions

To write a fraction in lowest terms

Words to learn

Fraction *a number that describes a part of a whole*

Numerator *the number above the fraction bar in a fraction*

Denominator *the number below the fraction bar in a fraction*

Equivalent fractions *fractions that have the same value*

Lowest terms *a fraction is in lowest terms if it has no common factor other than 1 in its numerator and denominator*

Vinny's Pizza delivered two large pizzas to a party. One pizza was divided into eight equal pieces. Diana had two slices of this pizza. The second pizza was divided into 12 equal pieces. Mimi had three slices of this pizza. Diana says that Mimi and she had the same amount of pizza. Is she right?

New Idea

A **fraction** (FRAK-shun) names a part of a whole. The fraction $\frac{3}{4}$ has two parts. In the first drawing below, the **numerator** (NOO-muhr-ayt-uhr), 3, tells how many parts are shaded, and the **denominator** (dee-NAHM-uh-nayt-uhr), 4, tells how many equal parts make up the whole. The numerator is always above the fraction bar. The denominator is always below the fraction bar.

Examples: What fraction of each drawing is shaded?

This rectangle is divided into 4 equal parts. Three of the parts are shaded. The fraction $\frac{3}{4}$ describes how much of the rectangle is shaded.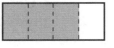

This rectangle is divided into 8 equal parts. Six of the parts are shaded. The fraction $\frac{6}{8}$ describes how much of the rectangle is shaded.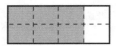

The rectangles are the same size. The shaded areas are the same size.

Fractions like $\frac{3}{4}$ and $\frac{6}{8}$ are called **equivalent fractions** (ee-KWIHV-uh-luhnt FRAK-shuhnz). Two fractions that are equivalent have the same value.

These diagrams show more pairs of equivalent fractions.

$\frac{1}{2} = \frac{4}{8}$

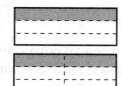

$\frac{1}{3} = \frac{2}{6}$

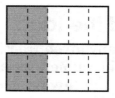

$\frac{2}{5} = \frac{4}{10}$

In a fraction, when the numerator and denominator are multiplied or divided by the same number, the new fraction is equivalent to the original fraction.

Example: In the problem about the pizza, Diana ate $\frac{2}{8}$ of the pizza. Mimi ate $\frac{3}{12}$.

Are $\frac{2}{8}$ and $\frac{3}{12}$ equivalent fractions?

$$\frac{2}{8} = \frac{(2 \div 2)}{(8 \div 2)} = \frac{1}{4} \qquad \frac{3}{12} = \frac{(3 \div 3)}{(12 \div 3)} = \frac{1}{4}$$

Since the fractions $\frac{2}{8}$ and $\frac{3}{12}$ are both equal to $\frac{1}{4}$, they are equivalent. So Diana and Mimi did eat the same amount of pizza.

✓**Check Your Understanding**

1. If either rectangle on page 72 was divided into 16 equal parts, how many parts would be shaded? _____

Focus on the Idea

A fraction is a number that names parts of a whole. Equivalent fractions are fractions that have the same value.

Practice

Shade the diagram to represent the fractional part. The first one is done for you.

2. $\frac{3}{8}$

3. $\frac{1}{2}$

4. $\frac{4}{5}$

5. $\frac{3}{10}$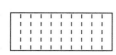

6. $\frac{5}{6}$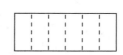

7. $\frac{2}{7}$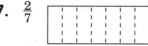

Are the two fractions equivalent? Write *yes* or *no*.

8. $\frac{2}{3}$ and $\frac{4}{6}$ _____

9. $\frac{3}{4}$ and $\frac{4}{5}$ _____

10. $\frac{2}{10}$ and $\frac{1}{5}$ _____

11. $\frac{5}{6}$ and $\frac{10}{12}$ _____

12. $\frac{3}{5}$ and $\frac{7}{9}$ _____

13. $\frac{15}{30}$ and $\frac{1}{2}$ _____

Extend the Idea

For any given fraction, there are many equivalent fractions. If the GCF of the numerator and denominator of a fraction is 1, that fraction is in **lowest terms** (LOH-uhst termz).

To write a fraction in lowest terms, follow these steps.

Step 1   Find the GCF of the numerator and the denominator.

Step 2   Divide the numerator and the denominator by the GCF.

Example: Write the fraction $\frac{6}{10}$ in lowest terms.

$\frac{6}{10}$ ←The GCF of 6 and 10 is 2.

$\frac{6}{10} = \frac{(6 \div 2)}{(10 \div 2)} = \frac{3}{5}$ ←Divide by the GCF.

The fraction $\frac{6}{10}$ in lowest terms is $\frac{3}{5}$ because the GCF of 3 and 5 is 1.

✓**Check the Math**

14. Phillip said that $\frac{8}{10}$ is equivalent to $\frac{7}{9}$ since $8 - 1 = 7$ and $10 - 1 = 9$. Is he correct? Explain your answer.

_____

_____

Practice

Write each fraction in lowest terms. The first one is done for you.

15. $\frac{12}{15} = $ _____ $\frac{4}{5}$

16. $\frac{20}{35}$ _____

17. $\frac{10}{12}$ _____

18. $\frac{6}{12}$ _____

19. $\frac{7}{8}$ _____

20. $\frac{42}{60}$ _____

21. $\frac{8}{12}$ _____

22. $\frac{14}{15}$ _____

23. $\frac{5}{15}$ _____

24. $\frac{40}{65}$ _____

25. $\frac{21}{24}$ _____

26. $\frac{25}{90}$ _____

Apply the Idea

27. Jordan has 36 cartons to unpack. He decides to break up his work time into three equal parts.

    a. How many cartons can he stack before his first rest break? _____

    b. What fractional part has he completed at each break?
    1st _____ 2nd _____ 3rd _____

28. A carpenter made several measurements, measuring in sixteenths of an inch. She needed to find equivalent fractions for the scale drawing she was making. Rewrite each of her measurements in lowest terms, if possible.

    a. Clearance between drawer and cabinet:
    $\frac{2}{16}$ inch _____

    b. Thickness of side of drawer: $\frac{4}{16}$ inch _____

    c. Diameter of hole for drawer knob: $\frac{5}{16}$ inch _____

    d. Thickness of plywood for shelving: $\frac{8}{16}$ inch _____

Write About It

29. Many people, such as carpenters, cooks, engineers, and architects, use fractional measurements in their work. List the fractional measurements you use. Then tell how and when you use them in your daily life.

Fractional Measurements I Use Most	How and When I Use Them

Finding the Least
Common Multiple

To find multiples of a number

To find the least common multiple of two or more numbers

To compare fractions

WORDS TO LEARN

Multiple *a number that is the product of a given number and any whole number*

Least common multiple (LCM) *the smallest number that is a multiple of two or more given numbers*

A sewing store has a box of ribbons on sale for $1 each. One ribbon is marked $\frac{3}{4}$ yard. Another is marked $\frac{2}{3}$ yard. Which ribbon is the better buy?

New Idea

To answer the question, you need to compare the pieces of ribbon. To do this, you must be able to compare, add, and subtract fractions. A **multiple** (MUL-tih-puhl) of a number is the product of that number and a whole number. The first four multiples of 3 are 3, 6, 9, and 12, because $1 \times 3 = 3$, $2 \times 3 = 6$, $3 \times 3 = 9$, and $4 \times 3 = 12$.

Any two numbers may have multiples that are the same, or common to them both. The **least common multiple** (leest KAHM-uhn MUL-tih-puhl) **(LCM)** is the smallest of the common multiples.

One way to find the least common multiple of two numbers is first to write the multiples of each number, circle the common multiples, and then choose the smallest of the common multiples.

Example: Find the LCM of 3 and 4.

Multiples of 3: 3, 6, 9, 12, 15, 18, 21, 24, 27, 30, 33, 36

Multiples of 4: 4, 8, 12, 16, 20, 24, 28, 32, 36

Common multiples of 3 and 4 are: 12, 24, 36, and so on.

The LCM of 3 and 4 is 12.

The LCM is used to find an equivalent fraction with a specific denominator.

Example: Compare the ribbons. Find the one that will give you more for your money.

Rewrite each of the fractions, $\frac{3}{4}$ and $\frac{2}{3}$, as an equivalent fraction with a common denominator. The LCM of 3 and 4 is 12. Find an equivalent fraction for $\frac{3}{4}$ and $\frac{2}{3}$ with 12 as the denominator.

$$\frac{3}{4} = \frac{?}{12} = \frac{(3 \cdot 3)}{(4 \cdot 3)} = \frac{9}{12}$$

$$\frac{2}{3} = \frac{?}{12} = \frac{(2 \cdot 4)}{(3 \cdot 4)} = \frac{8}{12}$$

To compare the ribbons in the sewing store, use the equivalent fractions. Since $\frac{3}{4} = \frac{9}{12}$ and $\frac{2}{3} = \frac{8}{12}$, the fraction $\frac{9}{12}$ is greater than the fraction $\frac{8}{12}$. So, the ribbon that is $\frac{3}{4}$ yd is longer than the one that is $\frac{2}{3}$ yd and is the better buy.

Focus on the Idea

The least common multiple (LCM) of a group of numbers is the smallest of the common multiples of the numbers. The LCM can be used to compare two fractions with different denominators.

Practice

Find the least common multiple. The first one is done for you.

1. 2, 4 _____4_____   **2.** 3, 5 _____   **3.** 2, 8 _____

4. 4, 5 _____   **5.** 12, 15 _____   **6.** 3, 4, 6 _____

Use the LCM to rewrite each pair of fractions as equivalent fractions with the same denominator. The first one is started for you.

7. $\frac{1}{3}, \frac{1}{2}$ ___$\frac{1}{3} = \frac{}{6}$___ ___$\frac{1}{2} = \frac{}{6}$___   **8.** $\frac{3}{4}, \frac{1}{2}$ _____ _____

9. $\frac{1}{4}, \frac{3}{8}$ _____ _____   **10.** $\frac{2}{5}, \frac{3}{10}$ _____ _____

Apply the Idea

11. A carpenter has drill bits for her drill marked in sixteenths of an inch. She needs a bit that will make a hole $\frac{3}{8}$ of an inch in diameter. Find a fraction equivalent to $\frac{3}{8}$ with a denominator of 16. _____

12. Which drill bit is larger, one that measures $\frac{1}{4}$ inch across or one that measures $\frac{3}{16}$ inch across? _____

Write About It

13. The LCM of two numbers is sometimes the product of the numbers. Give an example. Explain why this happens.

Chapter 4   Review

In This Chapter, You Have Learned

- To evaluate a numerical or variable expression containing exponents
- To identify prime and composite numbers and find the prime factors of a number
- To identify monomials, their coefficients, and numerical and variable factors of monomials
- To identify binomials, trinomials, polynomials, and constants, and simplify polynomials by combining like terms
- To find the greatest common factor of two or more numbers
- To write fractions, identify equivalent fractions, and write fractions in lowest terms
- To find multiples of a number, the least common multiple of two or more numbers, and to compare fractions

Words You Know

From the lists of "Words To Learn," choose the word or phrase that best completes each statement.

1. A(n) _____ is a product of numbers and variables.
2. A(n) _____ is the sum of two monomials.
3. The number 8 is a(n) _____ of 32 and 40.
4. The number -3 is the _____ of $-3y$.
5. A polynomial with three terms is called a(n) _____ .
6. The number 2 is the _____ of c in $8c^2$.

More Practice

Evaluate each expression.

7. $(-3)^2$ _____
8. $(-3)^3$ _____
9. 5^2 _____
10. $x^2 + 4$ if $x = 7$ _____
11. $3y^3$ if $y = -2$ _____

Write each number as a product of its prime factors.

12. $28 =$ _____
13. $32 =$ _____
14. $42 =$ _____
15. $45 =$ _____

What is the coefficient of each monomial?

16. $3x^5$ _____
17. $-4x^2y^4$ _____
18. $\frac{4z^2}{5}$ _____

Simplify, if possible.

19. $5a + 4 + 3a - 7 =$ _____

20. $4x^2 - 7x + 9x^2 + 5x =$ _____

Find the GCF for each pair of numbers.

21. 4, 14 _____   **22.** 10, 25 _____   **23.** 18, 24 _____

Write each fraction in lowest terms.

24. $\frac{32}{60}$ _____   **25.** $\frac{20}{45}$ _____

Find the LCM for each pair of numbers.

26. 2, 7 _____   **27.** 5, 30 _____

Rewrite each pair of fractions so they have the same denominator.

28. $\frac{1}{2}, \frac{3}{5}$ _____ _____   **29.** $\frac{3}{4}, \frac{1}{12}$ _____ _____

Problems You Can Solve

30. A contractor is designing a rectangular patio that must be 60 square feet. What are all the possible dimensions she can use, assuming that each dimension must be a whole number of feet?

_____

31. A box of 24 cans includes 5 cans that are crushed. What fractional part of the cans are crushed? _____

32. **For Your Portfolio** Draw a diagram showing two equivalent fractions. Write a paragraph describing how your drawing shows that the fractions are equivalent.

_____

_____

_____

Chapter 4   Practice Test

Evaluate each expression.

1. $8^2 + 7$ _____

2. $(-4)^3$ _____

3. $9x^3 + 6x$ if $x = 2$ _____

4. $100 - 3y^2$ if $y = 5$ _____

Write each number as a product of its prime factors.

5. $22 =$ _____

6. $40 =$ _____

Simplify, if possible.

7. $7x^3 + 5x^2 - 3x^3 + x^2 =$ _____

8. $b^4 + 6 + 9b^4 - 14 =$ _____

Find the GCF of each pair of numbers.

9. $14, 21$ _____

10. $10, 30$ _____

Write a fraction for the shaded part of each picture.

11.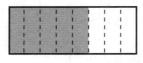

12.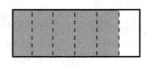

_____   _____

Write each fraction in lowest terms.

13. $\frac{12}{15}$ _____

14. $\frac{20}{24}$ _____

15. $\frac{30}{45}$ _____

Find the LCM for each pair of numbers.

16. $6, 10$ _____

17. $4, 18$ _____

Rewrite each pair of fractions so they have the same denominator.

18. $\frac{1}{4}, \frac{5}{6}$ _____ _____

19. $\frac{2}{5}, \frac{3}{15}$ _____ _____

Solve.

20. One gas station is $\frac{1}{2}$ mile from George's house. Another gas station is $\frac{3}{10}$ mile from his house. Which station is closer to his house? How do you know?

_____

_____

_____

Chapter 5

Solving Equations with Fractions

OBJECTIVES:

In this chapter, you will learn

- *To add fractions and mixed numbers*
- *To solve equations by adding fractions and mixed numbers*
- *To subtract fractions and mixed numbers*
- *To solve equations by subtracting fractions and mixed numbers*
- *To multiply fractions and mixed numbers*
- *To solve equations by multiplying fractions and mixed numbers*
- *To divide fractions and mixed numbers*
- *To solve equations by dividing fractions and mixed numbers*

The Case of the Missing Measuring Tools

Frieda is about to use these ingredients to make pancakes.

$2\frac{1}{2}$ c flour   1 egg

$\frac{1}{2}$ c sugar   2 tsp baking powder

1 c milk $\frac{1}{2}$ tsp salt

Frieda finds that she has only two measuring tools — a $\frac{1}{2}$-teaspoon measuring spoon and a $\frac{1}{4}$-cup measuring cup. Do you think Frieda can measure the ingredients using only these two tools?

Solving Equations by Adding Fractions

IN THIS LESSON, YOU WILL LEARN

To add fractions and mixed numbers

To solve equations by adding fractions and mixed numbers

WORDS TO LEARN

Common denominator *a common multiple of two or more denominators*

Improper fraction *a fraction in which the numerator is equal to or greater than the denominator*

Mixed number *a combination of a whole number and a fraction*

To make a sheet of plywood, a carpenter glues a layer of wood $\frac{1}{8}$-inch thick onto a board $\frac{1}{4}$-inch thick. What is the total thickness of the sheet?

New Idea

When two fractions have the same denominator, we say they have a **common denominator** (KAHM-uhn dee-NAHM-uh-nayt-uhr). To add two fractions that have a common denominator, add only the numerators. The denominator of the sum stays the same. Then write the sum in lowest terms, if necessary.

When two fractions have different denominators, you must change one or both to an equivalent fraction with like denominators.

Examples: Add. $\frac{1}{8} + \frac{3}{8}$

$$\frac{1}{8} + \frac{3}{8} = \frac{4}{8} = \frac{1}{2}$$

To find the total thickness of the sheet of plywood, add $\frac{1}{8}$ to $\frac{1}{4}$. First find a common denominator for the fractions. The least common multiple of 8 and 4 is 8, so rewrite each fraction with the denominator 8.

$$\frac{1}{8} = \frac{1}{8}$$
$$+\frac{1}{4} = \frac{2}{8}$$
$$\overline{\phantom{+\frac{1}{4} = }\frac{3}{8}}$$

The plywood is $\frac{3}{8}$-inch thick.

Solve the equation. $x - \frac{2}{3} = \frac{1}{6}$

$$x - \frac{2}{3} = \frac{1}{6}$$

$$x - \frac{2}{3} + \frac{2}{3} = \frac{1}{6} + \frac{2}{3} \quad \leftarrow \text{Add } \frac{2}{3} \text{ to both sides of the equation.}$$

$$x = \frac{1}{6} + \frac{4}{6} \quad \leftarrow \text{Write } \frac{2}{3} \text{ with a denominator of 6. Add.}$$

$$x = \frac{5}{6}$$

Check: $x - \frac{2}{3} = \frac{1}{6}$

$$\frac{5}{6} - \frac{2}{3} \overset{?}{=} \frac{1}{6} \quad \leftarrow \text{Substitute } \frac{5}{6} \text{ for } x.$$

$$\frac{5}{6} - \frac{4}{6} \overset{?}{=} \frac{1}{6} \quad \leftarrow \text{Write } \frac{2}{3} \text{ with a denominator of 6. Subtract.}$$

$$\frac{1}{6} = \frac{1}{6}$$

This checks, so the solution to the equation is $\frac{5}{6}$.

◣ Focus on the Idea

To add fractions that have the same denominators, add the numerators; the denominator remains the same. To add fractions with different denominators, change the fractions to equivalent fractions with the same denominator. Then add.

✓ Check Your Understanding

1. Add $\frac{2}{3}$ and $\frac{1}{5}$. First rewrite each fraction with the common denominator 15, then add.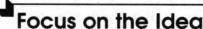

Practice

Add. Write the sum in lowest terms. The first two are done for you.

2. $\frac{1}{8} + \frac{1}{8} = \frac{2}{8} = \frac{1}{4}$ 3. $\frac{1}{3} + \frac{2}{9} = \frac{3}{9} + \frac{2}{9} = \frac{5}{9}$

4. $\frac{4}{9} + \frac{1}{3} =$ 5. $\frac{1}{4} + \frac{1}{2} =$

6. $\frac{1}{5} + \frac{1}{10} =$ 7. $\frac{1}{2} + \frac{1}{6} =$

8. $\frac{1}{3} + \frac{1}{4} =$ 9. $\frac{1}{3} + \frac{2}{15} =$

10. $\frac{2}{5} + \frac{1}{2} =$ 11. $\frac{1}{10} + \frac{1}{4} =$

Solve each equation. Write the solution in lowest terms.

12. $a - \frac{1}{3} = \frac{1}{5}$ 13. $y - \frac{1}{6} = \frac{5}{12}$

14. $-\frac{1}{5} + m = \frac{7}{10}$ 　　　　　　**15.** $f - \frac{3}{4} = \frac{1}{8}$

Extend the Idea

An **improper fraction** (ihm-prahp-uhr FRAK-shun) is a fraction in which the numerator is equal to or greater than the denominator. A **mixed number** (mikst NUM-buhr) is a combination of a whole number and a fraction. A mixed number can be rewritten as an improper fraction.

An improper fraction can be rewritten as a whole number or a mixed number. To rewrite an improper fraction, divide the numerator by the denominator and write any remainder as a fraction.

Examples: Rewrite $2\frac{1}{3}$ as an improper fraction.

$$2\frac{1}{3} = 2 + \frac{1}{3} = \frac{6}{3} + \frac{1}{3} = \frac{7}{3}$$

Rewrite $\frac{5}{2}$, $\frac{10}{5}$, and $\frac{6}{5}$ as mixed numbers or whole numbers.

$$\frac{5}{2} = 2\frac{1}{2} \qquad\qquad \frac{10}{5} = 2 \qquad\qquad \frac{6}{5} = 1\frac{1}{5}$$

To add mixed numbers, add the fraction parts, then add the whole-number parts. If the fraction parts have unlike denominators, first rename them using like denominators.

If the sum of the fraction parts of a mixed number is an improper fraction, first rewrite the improper fraction as a mixed number. Add, then write the sum in lowest terms.

Example: Add. $5\frac{3}{4} + 7\frac{5}{8}$

$$
\begin{array}{r}
5\frac{3}{4} = 5\frac{6}{8} \\
+7\frac{5}{8} = 7\frac{5}{8} \\
\hline
12\frac{11}{8} = 13\frac{3}{8}
\end{array}
$$

✓Check the Math

16. Louise has 5 yards of fabric. She wants to make a skirt that will take $2\frac{1}{2}$ yards of fabric and a shirt that will take $2\frac{3}{4}$ yards. Does she have enough fabric? How do you know?

_____

Practice

Add. Write each sum in lowest terms. The first one is done for you.

17. $1\frac{1}{4} + 2\frac{1}{4} =$ ___$3\frac{1}{2}$___ 　　　　**18.** $2\frac{5}{8} + 1\frac{1}{2} =$ _____

19. $8\frac{1}{2} + 4\frac{3}{4} =$ _____ 　　　　**20.** $9\frac{4}{7} + 10\frac{1}{2} =$ _____

21. $5\frac{1}{8} + 2\frac{3}{8} =$ _____ 　　　　**22.** $6\frac{2}{3} + 1\frac{1}{4} =$ _____

23. $15\frac{3}{7} + 21\frac{4}{7} = $ _____ **24.** $11\frac{1}{3} + 13\frac{4}{5} = $ _____

Solve each equation. Write the solution in lowest terms. Check your solutions. The first one is done for you.

25. $\quad x - 1\frac{1}{2} = 3\frac{1}{4}$ **26.** $\quad n - \frac{5}{3} = \frac{5}{12}$ **27.** $\quad 1\frac{1}{5} = m - \frac{4}{5}$

$$x - 1\frac{1}{2} + 1\frac{1}{2} = 3\frac{1}{4} + 1\frac{1}{2}$$
$$x = 3\frac{1}{4} + 1\frac{2}{4}$$
$$x = 4\frac{3}{4}$$

Check: $4\frac{3}{4} - 1\frac{1}{2} \overset{?}{=} 3\frac{1}{4}$
$$4\frac{3}{4} - 1\frac{2}{4} \overset{?}{=} 3\frac{1}{4}$$
$$3\frac{1}{4} = 3\frac{1}{4}$$

28. $2\frac{1}{3} + e = 4\frac{7}{9}$ **29.** $y - 1\frac{5}{6} = 2\frac{1}{4}$ **30.** $s - 1\frac{2}{3} = 7\frac{1}{2}$

Apply the Idea

31. A cabinet maker is using $\frac{3}{4}$-inch plywood to make a cabinet door. He will glue a $\frac{1}{8}$-inch-thick layer of veneer to the front of the door. What will be the total thickness of the door?

_____

32. Jane ran $\frac{1}{2}$ mile to the park and $\frac{3}{10}$ of a mile to the lake. How far was that? _____

33. Libby has two cabinets, one $24\frac{1}{2}$ inches wide and another $18\frac{1}{4}$ inches wide. They will be placed up against each other along one wall of Libby's room. What will the total width of the cabinets be? _____

Write About It

34. Make up a problem about a real situation that involves adding $\frac{7}{8}$ and $\frac{4}{3}$. Find the sum and explain what it means in your problem.

_____

_____

_____

◢5•2 Solving Equations by Subtracting Fractions

◢ **IN THIS LESSON, YOU WILL LEARN**

To subtract fractions and mixed numbers

To solve equations by subtracting fractions and mixed numbers

WORDS TO LEARN

Rename *to write a number in a different form*

Hidalgo has a piece of wood shelving that measures $3\frac{1}{4}$ feet. From it, he cuts a piece $1\frac{1}{2}$ feet long. How much shelving will he have left over?

New Idea

Fractions can be subtracted if they have the same denominator. To subtract two fractions that do not have the same denominator, find the least common multiple of the denominators. Then rewrite one or both of the fractions so they have the same denominator. Always express the difference in lowest terms.

To subtract mixed numbers, first subtract the fraction parts. Then subtract the whole-number parts. Sometimes you must **rename** (ree-NAYM) a mixed number, or write it in a different form, before you can subtract.

Examples: Subtract. $\frac{3}{4} - \frac{1}{8}$ Subtract. $7\frac{2}{3} - 2\frac{1}{4}$

$$\begin{array}{rcr} \frac{3}{4} &=& \frac{6}{8} \\ -\frac{1}{8} &=& -\frac{1}{8} \\ \hline && \frac{5}{8} \end{array} \qquad \begin{array}{rcr} 7\frac{2}{3} &=& 7\frac{8}{12} \\ -2\frac{1}{4} &=& -2\frac{3}{12} \\ \hline && 5\frac{5}{12} \end{array}$$

To find the amount of shelving Hidalgo had left over, subtract $1\frac{1}{2}$ from $3\frac{1}{4}$. The common denominator is 4. Rename $3\frac{1}{4}$ as $2\frac{5}{4}$ and $1\frac{1}{2}$ as $1\frac{2}{4}$ so you can subtract.

$$3\frac{1}{4} = 2 + 1 + \frac{1}{4} = 2 + \frac{4}{4} + \frac{1}{4} = 2\frac{5}{4}$$

$$\begin{array}{rcr} 3\frac{1}{4} &=& 2\frac{5}{4} \\ -1\frac{1}{2} &=& -1\frac{2}{4} \\ \hline && 1\frac{3}{4} \end{array}$$

There will be $1\frac{3}{4}$ feet of shelving left over.

Focus on the Idea

Subtracting fractions and mixed numbers is like adding fractions and mixed numbers. Before you subtract, be sure the fractions have a common denominator. You may have to rename a mixed number before you can subtract.

Practice

Subtract. Write each difference in lowest terms. The first two are done for you.

1. $\frac{7}{12} - \frac{5}{12} = \underline{\frac{2}{12} = \frac{1}{6}}$

2. $3\frac{3}{4} - 1\frac{1}{8} = \underline{3\frac{6}{8} - 1\frac{1}{8} = 2\frac{5}{8}}$

3. $\frac{5}{8} - \frac{1}{4} = $ _____

4. $5\frac{5}{6} - 1\frac{2}{3} = $ _____

5. $\frac{5}{6} - \frac{1}{6} = $ _____

6. $8\frac{2}{3} - 3\frac{1}{6} = $ _____

7. $\frac{9}{10} - \frac{3}{5} = $ _____

8. $4\frac{1}{3} - 1\frac{1}{2} = $ _____

9. $\frac{2}{3} - \frac{1}{4} = $ _____

10. $6\frac{1}{5} - 2\frac{7}{10} = $ _____

Solve each equation. Write the solution in lowest terms.

11. $m + \frac{1}{8} = \frac{5}{8}$

   $m = $ _____

12. $\frac{1}{3} + r = \frac{5}{6}$

   $r = $ _____

13. $\frac{6}{7} + \frac{2}{7} = x$

   $x = $ _____

14. $y + 2\frac{1}{4} = 5\frac{1}{2}$

   $y = $ _____

15. $\frac{3}{10} + c = \frac{3}{5}$

   $c = $ _____

16. $4\frac{1}{4} = f + 1\frac{7}{8}$

   $f = $ _____

Apply the Idea

17. A plumber has a $4\frac{1}{2}$-foot-long pipe. He cuts off a piece $1\frac{3}{4}$ feet long. How long is the piece that is left? _____

18. The opening for a drawer in a desk is $8\frac{1}{4}$ inches wide. The drawer needs a $\frac{1}{8}$-inch space on each side to slide properly. How wide can the drawer be? _____

Write About It

19. Use a ruler to draw a line $2\frac{1}{8}$ inches long. Mark off $1\frac{3}{4}$ inches of your line. Measure the remainder of the line. Then explain how to subtract the following: $2\frac{1}{8} - 1\frac{3}{4}$.

_____

5•3 Solving Equations by Multiplying Fractions

IN THIS LESSON, YOU WILL LEARN

To multiply fractions and mixed numbers

To solve equations by multiplying fractions and mixed numbers

WORDS TO LEARN

Acre *a special unit of area used in land measurements*

Area *measure of a flat region inside a figure*

Identity Property for Multiplication *a rule that states that any number multiplied by 1 equals itself*

An **acre** (AY-ker) is a special unit of area used in land measurements. An average-sized farm is 460 acres, or about $\frac{3}{4}$ of a square mile. A farmer has a rectangular cornfield that measures $\frac{3}{4}$ mile by $\frac{5}{6}$ mile. How many square miles is the cornfield?

New Idea

Area (AIR-ee-uh) is the measure of a flat region inside a figure. Area is measured in square units. To find the area of a rectangle, multiply the length by the width. To multiply fractions, multiply the numerators and then multiply the denominators. Write the product in lowest terms.

Example: Find the area of the farmer's cornfield.

If this rectangle represents a square mile, the area of the cornfield can be found by dividing it into 4 equal parts along its width and 6 equal parts along its length. The whole region is divided into 24 equal parts. Then $\frac{3}{4}$ of the width is shaded and $\frac{5}{6}$ of the length is shaded. Of the original 24 parts, 15 parts have double shading.

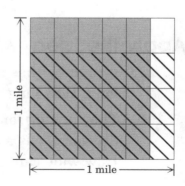

$$\frac{5}{6} \cdot \frac{3}{4} = \frac{15}{24}$$
$$= \frac{5}{8} \quad \leftarrow \text{lowest terms}$$

The area of the cornfield is $\frac{5}{8}$ of a square mile.

Any number divided by itself is 1, so each of $\frac{3}{3}$, $\frac{5}{5}$, and $\frac{6}{6}$ equals 1.

The number 1 has a special property: 1 times any number is that number. This is called the **Identity Property for Multiplication** (eye-DEHN-tuh-tee PRAHP-uhr-tee fawr mul-tuh-plih-KAY-shuhn).

Example: Multiply. $\frac{4}{15} \cdot \frac{9}{10}$

$$\frac{4}{15} \cdot \frac{9}{10} = \frac{4 \cdot 9}{15 \cdot 10}$$

$$= \frac{2 \cdot 2 \cdot 3 \cdot 3}{3 \cdot 5 \cdot 2 \cdot 5} \leftarrow \text{Factor numerators and denominators.}$$

$$= \frac{\cancel{2} \cdot 3 \cdot 2 \cdot 3}{\cancel{2} \cdot 3 \cdot 5 \cdot 5} \leftarrow \text{Rearrange the factors.}$$

$$= 1 \cdot 1 \cdot \frac{2 \cdot 3}{5 \cdot 5} \leftarrow \text{Replace } \frac{2}{2} \text{ with 1 and } \frac{3}{3} \text{ with 1. Multiply.}$$

$$= \frac{6}{25}$$

We can use this shortcut to express a fraction in lowest terms by canceling common factors that appear in the numerator and the denominator. We can also use the shortcut to multiply two fractions, by cancelling the common factors before multiplying.

Example: Use a shortcut to multiply $\frac{5}{8}$ and $\frac{6}{7}$.

$$\frac{5}{8} \cdot \frac{6}{7} = \frac{5 \cdot 2 \cdot 3}{2 \cdot 4 \cdot 7}$$

$$= \frac{\cancel{2} \cdot 5 \cdot 3}{\cancel{2} \cdot 4 \cdot 7} \quad (\frac{2}{2} = 1) \leftarrow \text{Cancel the 2's in the numerator and denominator.}$$

$$= \frac{15}{28}$$

✓Check Your Understanding

1. Do you need to find a common denominator in order to multiply two fractions? Explain your answer.

_____

Focus on the Idea

To multiply fractions, first multiply the numerators and then multiply the denominators. To express the product in lowest terms, divide the numerator and denominator by any common factors.

Practice

Multiply. Write the product in lowest terms. The first two are done for you.

2. $\frac{1}{3} \cdot \frac{1}{2} = \underline{\quad \frac{1}{6} \quad}$ 3. $\frac{7}{8} \cdot \frac{4}{5} = \underline{\quad \frac{28}{40} = \frac{7}{10} \quad}$ 4. $\frac{3}{5} \cdot \frac{2}{3} = \underline{\qquad}$

5. $\frac{5}{9} \cdot \frac{6}{7} =$ _____   **6.** $\frac{5}{7} \cdot \frac{14}{15} =$ _____   **7.** $\frac{3}{4} \cdot \frac{1}{9} =$ _____

8. $-\frac{2}{3} \cdot -\frac{9}{10} =$ _____   **9.** $\frac{5}{12} \cdot \frac{3}{20} =$ _____   **10.** $-\frac{4}{9} \cdot \frac{3}{4} =$ _____

Extend the Idea

To multiply whole numbers or mixed numbers, first change them to improper fractions. Every whole number can be written as a fraction with 1 as the denominator. Every mixed number can be thought of as a whole number plus a fraction. Change the mixed number to an improper fraction by finding a common denominator.

Examples: Change 12 to an improper fraction.

$$12 = \frac{12}{1}$$

Change $2\frac{1}{3}$ to an improper fraction.

$$2\frac{1}{3} = 2 + \frac{1}{3} = \frac{6}{3} + \frac{1}{3} = \frac{7}{3}$$

Find the product of $12 \cdot 2\frac{1}{3}$.

$$12 \cdot 2\frac{1}{3} = \frac{12}{1} \cdot \frac{7}{3}$$
$$= \frac{3 \cdot 2 \cdot 2 \cdot 7}{1 \cdot 3}$$
$$= \frac{\cancel{3} \cdot 2 \cdot 2 \cdot 7}{\cancel{3} \cdot 1}$$
$$= \frac{28}{1} = 28$$

To solve some equations with fractions, multiply both sides by the denominator of the variable fraction.

Example: Solve. $\frac{x}{4} = \frac{5}{6}$

$$\frac{x}{4} = \frac{5}{6} \qquad \leftarrow \text{Multiply both sides by 4.}$$
$$\frac{4}{1} \cdot \frac{x}{4} = \frac{5}{6} \cdot \frac{4}{1}$$
$$x = \frac{20}{6}$$
$$x = 3\frac{1}{3}$$

✓Check the Math

11. Jill said that $\frac{1}{2} \cdot \frac{3}{8}$ is $\frac{3}{4}$. Is she correct? Explain your answer.

_____

Practice

Find each product, and write it in lowest terms. The first one is done for you.

12. $\frac{3}{4} \cdot 5 = \frac{3}{4} \cdot \frac{5}{1}$ **13.** $7 \cdot 1\frac{1}{2} =$ **14.** $1\frac{1}{5} \cdot 2\frac{2}{3} =$

$\qquad = \frac{15}{4}$

$\qquad = 3\frac{3}{4}$

15. $2\frac{1}{5} \cdot 1\frac{1}{2} =$ 　　　　　**16.** $8 \cdot 3\frac{1}{2} =$ 　　　　　**17.** $1\frac{1}{8} \cdot 2\frac{1}{3} =$

Solve and check each equation. Write each solution in lowest terms. The first one has been done for you.

18. 　　$\frac{a}{3} = \frac{4}{5}$
　　　　$\frac{3}{1} \cdot \frac{a}{3} = \frac{4}{5} \cdot \frac{3}{1}$
　　　　$a = \frac{12}{5} = 2\frac{2}{5}$

19. $\frac{w}{4} = 2\frac{2}{3}$

20. $\frac{b}{2} = \frac{5}{8}$ 　　　　　　　　**21.** $\frac{e}{7} = 1\frac{3}{7}$

Apply the Idea

22. A rectangular field measures $\frac{7}{10}$ mile by $\frac{1}{2}$ mile. What is its area in square miles? _____

23. A room measures $3\frac{2}{3}$ yards by $4\frac{1}{2}$ yards. How many square yards of wall-to-wall carpeting are needed to cover the floor of the room? _____

24. The employees at a cleaning plant work three shifts. The day shift consists of $\frac{1}{3}$ of the 180 employees. How many employees are on the day shift? _____

25. A doctor found that $\frac{3}{4}$ of her patients live within 5 miles of her office. She has about 1,000 patients. About how many of her patients live within 5 miles of the office? _____

26. A carpenter cut a long board into 6 equal parts. Each part measured $1\frac{1}{3}$ yards. How long was the board before it was cut?

　　a. Underline the equation that could be used to solve this problem.
　　　　$6x = 1\frac{1}{3}$ 　　　$\frac{x}{6} = 1\frac{1}{3}$ 　　　$x - 6 = 1\frac{1}{3}$

　　b. Solve this problem using the equation. _____

Write About It

27. If you multiply two fractions, each of which is less than 1, the product will be less than each fraction. Explain why this is true.

_____

_____

►5•4 Solving Equations by Dividing Fractions

► IN THIS LESSON, YOU WILL LEARN

To divide fractions and mixed numbers

To solve equations by dividing fractions and mixed numbers

WORDS TO LEARN

Reciprocals *two numbers are reciprocals if their product is 1*

Boris has a piece of wood molding 3 feet long. He plans to use this molding to make a square picture frame with an outside edge that is $\frac{3}{4}$ foot long. Does he have enough molding to make the frame?

New Idea

Two numbers are **reciprocals** (rih-SIHP-ruh-kuhlz) if their product is 1. To write a reciprocal, invert, or switch, the positions of the numerator and denominator. To find the reciprocal of a mixed number, start by changing it to an improper fraction. To divide by a fraction or a mixed number, multiply by the reciprocal of the divisor.

Examples: Find the reciprocal of each of 3 and $1\frac{2}{3}$.

Since $3 = \frac{3}{1}$, the reciprocal of 3 is $\frac{1}{3}$.

To find the reciprocal of $1\frac{2}{3}$, first change it to an improper fraction: $1\frac{2}{3} = \frac{5}{3}$. The reciprocal of $1\frac{2}{3}$ is $\frac{3}{5}$.

You can use a diagram to solve Boris's problem.

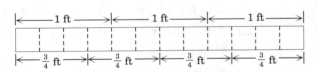

The diagram shows that 4 pieces, each $\frac{3}{4}$ foot long, can be cut from a 3-foot-long piece of molding.

You can also solve the problem by dividing 3 by $\frac{3}{4}$.

$3 \div \frac{3}{4} = 3 \cdot \frac{4}{3}$ ←Multiply by the reciprocal of $\frac{3}{4}$.

$\qquad = \frac{3}{1} \cdot \frac{4}{3}$ ←Multiply numerators. Multiply denominators.

$\qquad = \frac{12}{3}$ ←Simplify.

$\qquad = 4$

Boris will be able to cut 4 pieces, each $\frac{3}{4}$ foot long.

To solve an equation with a fraction, multiply both sides of the equation by the reciprocal of the fraction.

Example: Solve the equation. $\frac{4x}{5} = \frac{7}{8}$

$$\frac{4x}{5} = \frac{7}{8}$$

$$\frac{5}{4} \cdot \frac{4x}{5} = \frac{5}{4} \cdot \frac{7}{8} \qquad \leftarrow\text{Multiply both sides by } \frac{5}{4}.$$

$$x = \frac{35}{32}$$

$$x = 1\frac{3}{32} \qquad \leftarrow\text{Express the improper}$$
$$\text{fraction as a mixed number.}$$

◤Focus on the Idea

To divide by a fraction or mixed number, multiply by the reciprocal of that fraction or mixed number.

Practice

Find the reciprocal of each. The first one is done for you.

1. $\frac{2}{3}$ _____ $\frac{3}{2}$ _____

2. $1\frac{1}{2}$ _____

3. $-\frac{4}{5}$ _____

4. -14 _____

5. $\frac{1}{8}$ _____

6. $5\frac{1}{6}$ _____

Divide using reciprocals. Write the answers in lowest terms. The first one is done for you.

7. $\frac{2}{3} \div -\frac{4}{5} = \frac{2}{3} \cdot -\frac{5}{4} = \frac{1}{3} \cdot -\frac{5}{2} = -\frac{5}{6}$

8. $1\frac{1}{2} \div 2\frac{1}{3} =$

9. $-\frac{5}{8} \div 2 =$

10. $1\frac{1}{3} \div 2\frac{1}{4} =$

11. $-2\frac{1}{2} \div -1\frac{1}{4} =$

12. $5\frac{1}{4} \div 3 =$

Solve and check each equation. Write each solution in lowest terms.

13. $\frac{2x}{3} = 12$

14. $\frac{3b}{4} = 48$

15. $\frac{3h}{8} = 1\frac{3}{4}$

16. $\frac{5y}{6} = 3\frac{1}{3}$

Apply the Idea

17. How many pieces of ribbon $\frac{2}{3}$ yard long can be cut from a roll that is 60 yards long? _____

18. Linda has a board 8 feet long. She wants to make 3 shelves of equal length. How long should each shelf be? _____

✎ Write About It

19. Explain why dividing a number by 2 is the same as finding one half of that number. You might want to draw a picture to accompany your explanation.

_____

Chapter 5 Review

In This Chapter, You Have Learned

- To add fractions and mixed numbers
- To subtract fractions and mixed numbers
- To multiply fractions and mixed numbers
- To divide fractions and mixed numbers
- To solve one-step equations that include fractions

Words You Know

From the lists of "Words to Learn," choose the word or phrase that best completes each statement.

1. To add or subtract two fractions, the fractions must have a(n) _____.

2. The _____ states that any number multiplied by 1 is itself.

3. A fraction in which the numerator is equal to or greater than the denominator is called a(n) _____.

4. A number that has a whole number part and a fraction part is called a(n) _____.

5. Two numbers whose product is 1 are _____.

More Practice

Add or subtract. Write each answer in lowest terms.

6. $\frac{2}{7} + \frac{3}{7} =$ _____

7. $\frac{9}{10} - \frac{1}{5} =$ _____

8. $\frac{1}{4} + \frac{3}{8} =$ _____

9. $\frac{5}{8} - \frac{1}{2} =$ _____

10. $2\frac{1}{3} + 3\frac{1}{4} =$ _____

11. $4\frac{3}{4} - 1\frac{1}{8} =$ _____

12. $1\frac{7}{8} + 5\frac{3}{4} =$ _____

13. $5\frac{1}{3} - 2\frac{5}{6} =$ _____

Multiply or divide. Write each answer in lowest terms.

14. $\frac{2}{5} \cdot \frac{1}{3} =$ _____

15. $\frac{4}{5} \div \frac{1}{10} =$ _____

16. $\frac{5}{6} \cdot \frac{1}{2} =$ _____

17. $\frac{3}{4} \div \frac{1}{2} =$ _____

18. $\frac{3}{5} \cdot \frac{10}{27} =$ _____

19. $\frac{5}{8} \div \frac{1}{4} =$ _____

20. $1\frac{1}{2} \cdot 2\frac{1}{3} =$ _____

21. $\frac{2}{3} \div \frac{5}{6} =$ _____

22. $2\frac{5}{8} \cdot 3\frac{2}{3} =$ _____

23. $1\frac{3}{8} \div 2\frac{1}{5} =$ _____

Solve each equation. Write the solution in lowest terms.

24. $x + \frac{1}{3} = \frac{5}{6}$　　　　　　**25.** $\frac{m}{8} = 1\frac{3}{4}$

　　　　$x = $ _____　　　　　$m = $ _____

26. $b - \frac{3}{5} = \frac{7}{10}$　　　　　**27.** $\frac{3g}{4} = 2\frac{1}{2}$

　　　　$b = $ _____　　　　　$g = $ _____

Problems You Can Solve

28. A window is $3\frac{1}{2}$ feet high. There is molding above and below the window. Each piece of molding is $\frac{1}{3}$ foot high. A curtain is needed to cover the window and both moldings. How long should the curtain be? _____

29. In the problem on page 81, Frieda has a $\frac{1}{2}$ teaspoon and $\frac{1}{4}$ cup for measuring.

　a. How many $\frac{1}{4}$ cups of flour would she need to measure out $2\frac{1}{2}$ cups of flour? _____

　b. How many $\frac{1}{2}$ teaspoons of baking powder would she need to measure out 2 teaspoons of baking powder? _____

30. **For Your Portfolio**　Find a recipe that you might want to make. Assume you only have $\frac{1}{4}$ teaspoon and $\frac{1}{2}$ cup for measuring. Rewrite the recipe and tell how many $\frac{1}{4}$ teaspoons or $\frac{1}{2}$ cups you would need of each item.

Recipe for:

Ingredients:

_____　_____

_____　_____

_____　_____

Instructions:

Chapter 5　Practice Test

Calculate. Write each answer in lowest terms.

1. $\frac{3}{10} + \frac{1}{10} =$ _____

2. $\frac{3}{5} \cdot \frac{3}{4} =$ _____

3. $\frac{3}{7} + \frac{4}{7} =$ _____

4. $\frac{2}{7} \cdot \frac{5}{8} =$ _____

5. $2\frac{1}{4} + 3\frac{5}{8} =$ _____

6. $1\frac{2}{3} \cdot 2\frac{1}{10} =$ _____

7. $3\frac{5}{6} + 2\frac{2}{3} =$ _____

8. $2\frac{1}{5} \cdot 3\frac{1}{3} =$ _____

9. $4\frac{1}{2} - 2\frac{1}{8} =$ _____

10. $1\frac{5}{6} \div 2\frac{1}{4} =$ _____

11. $5\frac{1}{3} - 2\frac{1}{2} =$ _____

12. $8 \div 3\frac{1}{7} =$ _____

Solve each equation. Write the solution in lowest terms.

13. $a - \frac{1}{9} = \frac{1}{3}$

14. $x + \frac{4}{5} = \frac{5}{6}$

15. $\frac{t}{6} = 1\frac{1}{3}$

Solve.

16. How many $2\frac{1}{2}$-yard pieces of cable can be cut from a spool containing 50 yards of cable? _____

17. June had 5 yards of fabric. She used $2\frac{3}{8}$ yards to make a skirt. How many yards did she have left? _____

18. A stock price opened at $33\frac{1}{4}$ at the beginning of the day. It closed $1\frac{1}{2}$ points higher. What was the closing price of the stock? _____

19. A car's gas tank holds 20 gallons. If the tank is exactly $\frac{3}{4}$ full, how many gallons of fuel are in the tank? _____

20. If a room measures $10\frac{1}{3}$ yards by $8\frac{1}{2}$ yards, how many square yards of carpeting will be needed to cover the floor?

_____

Chapter 6

Solving Equations with Decimals

OBJECTIVES:

In this chapter, you will learn

- *To write a decimal to represent a value*
- *To compare decimals*
- *To add, subtract, multiply, and divide decimals*
- *To read a decimal*
- *To change decimals to fractions and fractions to decimals*
- *To solve equations with decimals*

You may have noticed that Olympic events often are timed in decimals of a second. This chart shows the winning times for the men's 100-meter backstroke during the summer Olympic games.

Year	Time	Year	Time
1908	1 minute 24.6 seconds	1956	1 minute 2.2 seconds
1912	1 minute 21.2 seconds	1960	1 minute 1.9 seconds
1920	1 minute 15.2 seconds	1968	58.7 seconds
1924	1 minute 13.2 seconds	1972	56.58 seconds
1928	1 minute 8.2 seconds	1976	55.49 seconds
1932	1 minute 8.6 seconds	1980	56.53 seconds
1936	1 minute 5.9 seconds	1984	55.79 seconds
1948	1 minute 6.4 seconds	1988	55.05 seconds
1952	1 minute 5.4 seconds	1992	53.98 seconds

As you read this chart, what are some of the things you notice about the times for this Olympic event? Why do you think decimals are used to measure time at many sports events?

Finding Equivalent Decimals and Fractions

◢ **IN THIS LESSON, YOU WILL LEARN**

To write a decimal to represent a value

To read a decimal

To compare decimals

To change decimals to fractions and fractions to decimals

WORDS TO LEARN

Micrometer *a device used to measure very small objects*

Decimal *a number that represents a fraction with a denominator that is a power of ten*

Equivalent decimals *two decimals with the same value*

Machinists need to measure the objects they make. A **micrometer** (my-KRAHM-uht-uhr) is a device used to measure very small objects. A machinist might find that the width of a nail is 0.125 inch. How could you describe the size of this measurement?

New Idea

A **decimal** (DEHS-uh-muhl) is a number that represents a fraction with a denominator that is a power of ten, such as $\frac{1}{10}$, $\frac{1}{100}$, $\frac{1}{1,000}$, and so on. A decimal whose value is less than 1 is written with a decimal point and digits to the right of the decimal point and a zero to the left. A decimal whose value is greater than 1 has digits both to the right and to the left of the decimal point.

Examples: Read these decimals: 2.4 and 0.053

The decimal 2.4 is read "two *and* four tenths."

(Say "and" when you get to the decimal point.)

The decimal 0.053 is read "fifty-three thousandths."

Hundreds	Tens	Ones	.	Tenths	Hundredths	Thousandths
		2	.	4		
		0	.	0	5	3

The square at the right represents one unit, or the whole number 1. When the unit is divided into ten equal parts, each part is one tenth of the unit. Notice that $\frac{1}{10}$ of the unit is shaded. This can be written as the decimal 0.1.

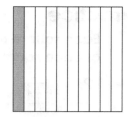

The whole number 1 can be divided into 100 parts. Ten of the 100 squares are shaded at the right. Notice that $\frac{10}{100}$ are shaded. This can be written as the decimal 0.10.

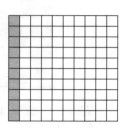

Equivalent decimals (ee-KWIHV-uh-luhnt DEHS-uh-muhlz) have the same value. The decimals 0.1 and 0.10 are equivalent decimals. Zeros added to the far right of a decimal point do not change the value of the decimal. Equivalent decimals are useful when comparing decimals.

Examples: Write decimals that are equivalent to 3.2.

The decimals 3.20 and 3.200 are equivalent to 3.2.

Compare 0.11 and 0.8.

Since 0.11 has two decimal places, rewrite 0.8 as an equivalent decimal with two decimal places.

0.8 = 0.80   Eight tenths is equivalent to eighty hundredths.

0.11 < 0.80   Eleven hundredths is less than eighty hundredths.

0.11 < 0.8   So, eleven hundredths is less than eight tenths.

✓ **Check Your Understanding**

1. Is a micrometer reading of 0.125 inches greater than or less than 0.25 inches? Explain your answer.

_____

_____

_____

◤ **Focus on the Idea**

A decimal is a number that represents a fraction or mixed number with a denominator that is a power of ten. Two decimals are equivalent if they have the same value.

Practice

Each square represents 1 whole. Write a decimal for the shaded part of each square. The first one is done for you.

2.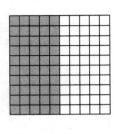

_____0.50_____

3.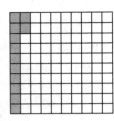

_____

Write < or > to compare each pair of decimals. The first one is done for you.

4. 0.7 __>__ 0.3

5. 0.14 _____ 0.2

6. 2.3 _____ 23

7. 0.35 _____ 0.035

8. 0.6 _____ 0.61

9. 0.4 _____ 0.27

Are the pairs of decimals equivalent? Write *yes* or *no*.

10. 0.2 and 0.02 _____

11. 0.4 and 0.400 _____

12. 1.04 and 1.0400 _____

13. 0.005 and 0.050 _____

Extend the Idea

Most decimals can be written as fractions. The way you read a decimal helps you identify the numerator and the denominator of the equivalent fraction.

When possible, rewrite the fraction in lowest terms.

Examples: Write 0.5 and 0.04 as fractions.

$$0.5 \quad \leftarrow \text{Read "five tenths." Write } \tfrac{5}{10}.$$

$$0.04 \quad \leftarrow \text{Read "four hundredths." Write } \tfrac{4}{100}.$$

Write 0.5 and 0.04 as fractions in lowest terms.

$$0.5 = \tfrac{5}{10} = \tfrac{1}{2}$$
$$0.04 = \tfrac{4}{100} = \tfrac{1}{25}$$

All fractions can be written as decimals. To change a fraction to a decimal, divide the numerator by the denominator. Some fractions have decimal patterns that repeat.

Examples: Write $\tfrac{3}{4}$ and $\tfrac{1}{3}$ as decimals.

$$\tfrac{3}{4} = 4)\overline{3.00} \quad\quad \tfrac{1}{3} = 3)\overline{1.00}$$

$$\phantom{\tfrac{3}{4} = 4)}0.75 \quad\quad\quad\quad 0.33...$$

The dots show that, as long as you keep on dividing, 3's will repeat.

So, $\frac{3}{4} = 0.75$.　　So, $\frac{1}{3} = 0.\overline{33}$. A bar indicates repeating digits.

✓ Check the Math

14. Carl says that the decimal for $\frac{1}{8}$ is 0.12. Is he correct? Explain your answer.

_____

Practice

Write each decimal as a fraction in lowest terms. The first one is done for you.

15. $0.09 = \dfrac{9}{100}$　　16. $0.6 =$ _____

17. $0.75 =$ _____　　18. $0.014 =$ _____

19. $0.12 =$ _____　　20. $1.2 =$ _____

Write each fraction as a decimal. Place a bar over any digits that repeat indefinitely.

21. $\frac{4}{5} =$ _____　　22. $\frac{5}{8} =$ _____

23. $\frac{3}{50} =$ _____　　24. $\frac{1}{6} =$ _____

25. $\frac{6}{25} =$ _____　　26. $\frac{4}{9} =$ _____

Apply the Idea

27. The diameter of a circular hole is 0.03 meter. Which of these is the greatest possible pipe diameter that will fit into the hole: 0.2 meter, 0.023 meter, 0.032 meter, 0.019 meter, or 0.027 meter? _____

28. The outer diameter of a pipe is $\frac{1}{2}$ inch. A micrometer indicates that the inner diameter is $\frac{5}{16}$ inch. Change the fractions to decimals to compare diameters. Which diameter is greater? _____

✎ Write About It

29. Write $\frac{1}{2}$, $\frac{2}{3}$, $\frac{1}{4}$, $\frac{3}{5}$, and $\frac{1}{6}$ as decimals. Find the factors of the denominators. Which of the fractions is a repeating decimal? How do you predict whether a fraction is a repeating decimal?

_____

_____

▸6•2 Adding Decimals

IN THIS LESSON, YOU WILL LEARN
To add decimals
To solve equations by adding decimals

WORDS TO LEARN
Vertical form *the alignment of two or more decimals so that their decimal points and place values are lined up vertically*

In a grocery store, the weight of meat is marked in decimal form. Eric has a recipe he wants to make that calls for 4.5 pounds of chicken. At the store, he finds packages that weigh 2.36 pounds, 1.94 pounds, 1.65 pounds, and 2.8 pounds. Which packages should he buy?

New Idea

Adding decimals is like adding whole numbers. Before you can add decimals, you must be sure they are written in **vertical form** (VER-tih-kuhl fawrm) so that their decimal points and place values are lined up vertically.

Example: Find the sum of 2.8 and 1.94.

$$
\begin{array}{r}
2.80 \\
+\ 1.94 \\
\hline
4.74
\end{array}
$$

← Add a zero to the right of the 8.

← Then add.

Some equations can be solved by adding decimals.

Example: After 2.5 meters of cloth were cut from a bolt, 2.78 meters were left. How much cloth had been on the bolt before the cloth was cut?

Write an equation.

Let x represent the amount of cloth originally on the bolt. Then, $x - 2.5 = 2.78$ is an equation for the problem.

$$x - 2.5 = 2.78$$

$$x - 2.5 + 2.5 = 2.78 + 2.5 \quad \leftarrow \text{Add 2.5 to both sides}$$
$$x = 5.28 \quad\quad\quad\quad \text{of the equation.}$$

There were 5.28 meters of cloth on the bolt originally.

Focus on the Idea

Before adding decimals, write them vertically so that their decimal points align.

Practice

Add. The first one is done for you.

1. $\begin{array}{r} 0.4 \\ +\ 0.3 \\ \hline 0.7 \end{array}$

2. $\begin{array}{r} 4.6 \\ 2.34 \\ +\ 1.8 \\ \hline \end{array}$

3. $\begin{array}{r} 5.5 \\ 11.902 \\ +\ 9.87 \\ \hline \end{array}$

Rewrite in vertical form, then add.

4. $0.145 + 8.9 + 23.67$

5. $7.02 + 3.9 + 0.03$

6. $0.094 + 0.15 + 3.296$

7. $24.36 + 32.9 + 8.783$

Solve each equation. The first one is done for you.

8. $m - 0.8 = 3.2$

    $m - 0.8 + 0.8 = 3.2 + 0.8$

    $m = 4.0$

9. $n - 0.3 = 4$

    $n =$

10. $w - 2.8 = 7.6$

    $w =$

11. $y - 3.52 = 5.1$

    $y =$

Apply the Idea

12. The hospital cafeteria has one bag of flour that weighs 1.2 kilograms and one that weighs 3.9 kilograms. Is there enough flour for a cookie recipe that calls for 5.25 kilograms?

    _____

Write About It

13. Decimals are used all the time. Name four uses of decimals. Work with a partner.

    _____

    _____

6•3 Subtracting Decimals

In this lesson, you will learn

To subtract decimals

To solve equations by subtracting decimals

Words to learn

Dowels *small, round rods used to stabilize a larger structure*

Carpenters use wooden joints to add support to the furniture they make. Small rods, called **dowels** (DOW-uhlz), fit into small holes to hold the pieces together.

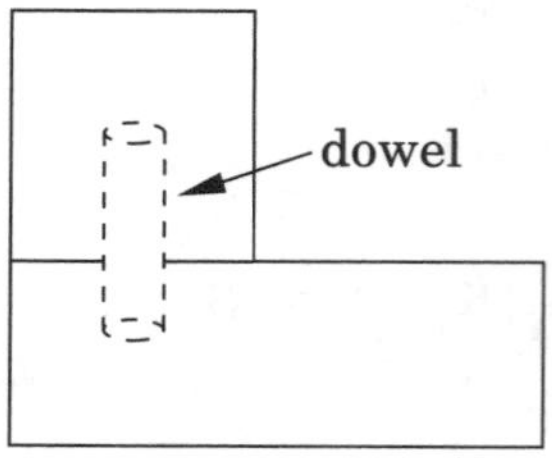

A carpenter has one dowel that is 30 centimeters long. She cuts it into two pieces to make a dowel joint. One piece is 10.4 centimeters. How long is the second piece?

New Idea

Subtracting decimals is like subtracting whole numbers. Be sure decimal points are aligned before you subtract. Sometimes you may need to rewrite problems using equivalent decimals.

Examples: Find the length of the second piece of the dowel by subtracting.

30.0	← Rewrite 30 as 30.0.
− 10.4	← Then subtract.
19.6	← The second piece is 19.6 cm long.

A pharmacist adds 2.3 milliliters of an antibiotic to a mixture. The total amount of the solution is 4.7 milliliters. How much solution had been in the test tube before the antibiotic was added?

Let y = the original amount of mixture.

Use the equation $y + 2.3 = 4.7$ to solve this problem.

$$y + 2.3 = 4.7$$
$$y + 2.3 - 2.3 = 4.7 - 2.3$$
$$y = 2.4$$

The test tube originally had 2.4 mL of solution.

Focus on the Idea

Subtract decimals the same way you subtract whole numbers. Align decimal points. If necessary, write equivalent decimals before you subtract.

Practice

Subtract. The first one is done for you.

1.   0.8
      − 0.5
      ———
       0.3

2.   12.1
      − 9.23
      ———

3.   7
      − 5.13
      ———

Rewrite in vertical form, then subtract.

4. $2.4 - 1.1$

5. $20.5 - 3.74$

6. $9 - 8.26$

Solve each equation. The first one is done for you.

7. $a + 2.8 = 5$

$a + 2.8 - 2.8 = 5 - 2.8$

$a = 2.2$

8. $b + 4.12 = 7.3$

$b =$

9. $q + 6 = 8.5$

$q =$

10. $h + 3.4 = 4.2$

$h =$

Apply the Idea

11. Jim buys a shirt for $13.50. How much change should he get from $20? _____

12. A hamburger weighs 6.3 ounces before cooking. After cooking, it weighs 4.7 ounces. How much weight was lost in cooking? _____

Write About It

13. Explain how subtracting decimals is like subtracting fractions. Explain how it is different.

_____

_____

▸6•4 Multiplying Decimals

▸ **IN THIS LESSON, YOU WILL LEARN**

To multiply decimals

To solve equations by multiplying decimals

WORDS TO LEARN

Factor *a number that is multiplied by another number to produce a product*

Carpeting usually sells by the square yard. Mrs. Fiorio buys 7.5 square yards of carpeting for her bedroom. The carpeting is priced at $18.50 per square yard. How much will the carpeting cost?

New Idea

To multiply a decimal by a whole number, first multiply the numbers. Then place the decimal point in the product to match the number of decimal places in the decimal **factor** (FAK-tuhr). (See Lesson 4•5.)

Example: 4.9   ←1 decimal place in factor

$\underline{\times\ 3}$

14.7   ←1 decimal place in product

To multiply decimals, first multiply the numbers. Then place the decimal point in the product to match the number of decimal places in the two factors.

Examples: Multiply 6.2 by 3.5, and 0.06 by 1.2.

6.2 ←1 decimal place	0.06 ←2 decimal places
$\underline{\times\ 3.5}$ ←1 decimal place	$\underline{\times\ 1.2}$ ←1 decimal place
3 10	12
$\underline{18\ 60}$	$\underline{\quad 60}$
21.70 ←2 decimal places	0.072 ←3 decimal places
	↑ This zero is a placeholder.

You can multiply decimals to solve some equations.

Example: Solve. $\frac{x}{0.4} = 3.2$

$$\frac{x}{0.4} = 3.2$$

$$(0.4)(\tfrac{x}{0.4}) = (0.4)(3.2) \quad \leftarrow \text{Multiply both sides by 0.4.}$$

$$x = 1.28 \qquad \leftarrow 2 \text{ decimal places}$$

◤ Focus on the Idea

To multiply two decimals, multiply the numbers, then place the decimal point in the product. The number of decimal places in the product is the total number of decimal places in the two factors.

Practice

Multiply. The first two are done for you.

1.
$$\begin{array}{r} 12 \\ \times\ 0.3 \\ \hline 3.6 \end{array}$$

2.
$$\begin{array}{r} 4.7 \\ \times\ 3.8 \\ \hline 376 \\ 1410 \\ \hline 17.86 \end{array}$$

3.
$$\begin{array}{r} 0.06 \\ \times\ 0.04 \\ \hline \end{array}$$

4. 93×0.22

5. 7.5×0.13

6. 6.25×0.008

Solve each equation.

7. $\frac{f}{0.2} = 45$

8. $\frac{g}{0.5} = 62$

9. $\frac{k}{1.5} = 2.8$

Apply the Idea

10. Look back at page 106. How much will Mrs. Fiorio pay for the carpeting? _____

11. The diagram shows the dimensions of a room in Mr. Clarke's store.

    a. Find the area in square yards. (Hint: Divide the room into two rectangles.)

    _____

    b. Find the cost of carpeting this room at $24.25 a square yard. _____

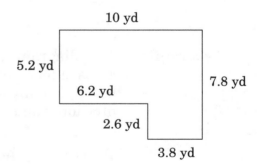

✎ Write About It

12. Use fractions to show that $0.9 \times 0.7 = 0.63$. Explain how the multiplication of decimals and fractions are similar.

_____

_____

_____

◢6•5 Dividing Decimals

Jorge is a carpenter helping to restore an old building. He must repair the wooden floors. He has some large boards that each measure 11.5 board feet. A **board foot** (BOHRD foot) is a unit for measuring lumber that is equal to 12 inches by 12 inches by 1 inch. Jorge needs floor planks that each measure 4 board feet to repair the damaged flooring. How many floor planks, 4 board feet in length, can Jorge cut from each large board?

New Idea

When dividing a decimal by a whole number, place the decimal point in the quotient directly above the decimal point in the dividend. Add zeros to the right of the dividend, until the remainder is zero, or until you can round the quotient to a given place.

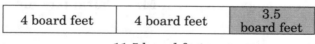

| 4 board feet | 4 board feet | 3.5 board feet |

11.5 board feet

Example: This diagram shows that two planks that measure 4 board feet can be cut from one 11.5-board foot board, leaving a remaining piece. Using long division, you can divide 11.5 by 4 as follows:

$$
\begin{array}{r}
2.875 \\
4\overline{)11.500} \\
-8\\
\overline{35}\\
-32\\
\overline{30}\\
-28\\
\overline{20}\\
-20\\
\overline{0}
\end{array}
$$

← Quotient

← Add two zeros to the dividend.

The quotient 2.875 shows that 2 whole planks can be cut from the large board, leaving a fractional part.

The decimal 0.875 is the fractional remainder:
$0.875 \times 4 = 3.5$, so 3.5 board feet are left.

Sometimes a quotient is a very long decimal. You can round the quotient to any given place. In a word problem, use the context of the problem to decide about rounding the quotient.

Remember

To round to a given place, look at the digit to the right of that place. If the digit to the right is 5 or more, add 1 to the rounding place. Drop the rest of the digits. If the digit to the right is less than 5, drop all digits to the right of the rounding place.

Example: When 12.8 is divided by 3, the quotient is 4.267. Rounded to the nearest tenth, the quotient is 4.3.

✓**Check Your Understanding**

1. How many planks that measure 3 board feet could Jorge cut from each 11.5-board foot board? _____

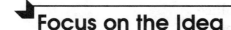**Focus on the Idea**

When you divide a decimal by a whole number, divide the same way you divide whole numbers. Be sure to put the decimal point in the quotient directly above the decimal point in the dividend.

Practice

Find the quotient. The first one is done for you.

2.
```
    1.57
 4)6.28
  -4
   22
  -20
    28
   -28
     0
```

3. $9)\overline{3.69}$

4. $7)\overline{4.55}$

5. $0.624 \div 8$

6. $115.2 \div 32$

7. $18.816 \div 12$

Divide. Round each quotient to the nearest tenth.

8. $20.6 \div 5$

9. $10.8 \div 32$

10. $6.805 \div 15$

Divide. Round each quotient to the nearest hundredth.

11. $95.09 \div 3$ 　　　　**12.** $1.3 \div 52$ 　　　　**13.** $0.783 \div 15$

Extend the Idea

In any division problem, when the divisor and the dividend are multiplied by the same number, the quotient remains the same. That is why the quotients for the following division problems are all the same:

$$8 \div 2 = 4 \qquad 80 \div 20 = 4 \qquad 800 \div 200 = 4$$

To make it easier to divide a decimal by a decimal, change the problem. Make the divisor a whole number by multiplying the divisor and the dividend by a power of ten, such as 10, 100, or 1,000. You can use these shortcuts for multiplying by powers of ten.

To multiply by	Move the decimal point to the right
10	1 place
100	2 places
1,000	3 places

Example:　Divide 0.65 by 0.5.

Start by multiplying both 0.65 and 0.5 by 10. This will change the problem so that it will have the same quotient, but the divisor will be a whole number:

$$0.5 \times 10 = 5.0 \text{ and } 0.65 \times 10 = 6.5$$

$$0.5\overline{)0.65} = 5\overline{)6.5}^{\,1.3}$$

You can solve equations with decimals.

Example:　Solve $0.3x = 4.2$.

$$0.3x = 4.2$$

$$\frac{0.3x}{0.3} = \frac{4.2}{0.3} \quad \leftarrow \text{Divide each side by 0.3.}$$

$$x = 14$$

✓Check the Math

14. Al divided 0.8 by 0.2 and got the quotient 0.4. Is he correct? Explain your answer.

_____

_____

Practice

Divide. The first one is done for you.

15.
$$
\begin{array}{r}
23.2 \\
0.4\overline{)9.28} \\
\underline{8} \\
12 \\
\underline{-12} \\
08 \\
\underline{-8} \\
0
\end{array}
$$

16. $1.8\overline{)6.12}$

17. $0.04\overline{)56.2}$

18. $0.21\overline{)4.2}$

19. $0.12\overline{)0.384}$

20. $0.61\overline{)88.45}$

Solve each equation.

21. $2a = 3.1$

22. $9b = 0.432$

23. $0.5x = 1.2$

24. $0.08y = 64$

25. $1.5e = 0.9$

26. $2.5f = 0.04$

Apply the Idea

27. A sack of flour has a mass of 8.5 kilograms. It is divided into five equal batches. What is the mass of each batch?

_____

28. Grant drove 275.2 miles on 11.2 gallons of gasoline. How many miles per gallon to the nearest tenth did his car get?

_____

29. A box of cereal weighs 13.5 ounces. If a serving size is 1.5 ounces, how many servings are in the box? _____

✏ Write About It

30. Does your calculator round quotients? Explain what your calculator does with a quotient that is too long for the display. Try 2 ÷ 3 on your calculator.

_____

_____

Chapter 6   Review

In This Chapter, You Have Learned
- To read and write decimals
- To compare decimals
- To change decimals to fractions and fractions to decimals
- To add, subtract, multiply and divide decimals
- To solve equations with decimals

Words You Know

From the lists of "Words to Learn," choose the word or phrase that best completes each statement.

1. Two decimals that have the same value are _____ decimals.
2. To write decimals vertically by aligning the decimal points is to put them in _____.
3. A(n) _____ is a number multiplied by another number to get a product.
4. A(n) _____ is a number that represents a fraction with a denominator that is a power of ten.

More Practice

Write a decimal for each diagram.

5.

6.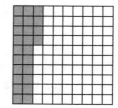

_____   _____

Compare. Use < or >.

7. 0.4 _____ 0.38   8. 2.03 _____ 2.1   9. 0.52 _____ 0.06

Change each fraction to a decimal.

10. $\frac{1}{4}$ = _____   11. $\frac{5}{6}$ = _____   12. $\frac{4}{5}$ = _____

Add or subtract.

13. $5.4 + 17.8$ = _____   14. $11.7 + 2.9$ = _____

15. $8.3 - 1.7$ = _____   16. $0.9 - 0.1$ = _____

17. $23.5 + 2.98 + 42$ = _____   18. $7 - 2.7$ = _____

Multiply or divide.

19. $0.3 \times 0.6 =$ _____   **20.** $8.2 \times 0.7 =$ _____

21. $4.2 \times 0.005 =$ _____   **22.** $2.1 \div 7 =$ _____

23. $4.5 \div 0.15 =$ _____   **24.** $72.48 \div 1.2 =$ _____

Solve each equation.

25. $a + 0.6 = 1.34$ **26.** $b - 8.2 = 5.6$

$a =$ $b =$

27. $x - 9.1 = 0.37$ **28.** $y - 0.003 = 5.2$

$x =$ $y =$

29. $2g = 9.3$ **30.** $\frac{h}{5} = 1.24$

$g =$ $h =$

Problems You Can Solve

31. Barry buys three packages of chicken. They weigh 2.31 pounds, 2.47 pounds, and 3.02 pounds. Find the weight of the three packages. _____

32. Gasoline costs $1.47 per gallon. How much will 12.5 gallons cost? _____

33. A piece of wood molding 4.02 meters long is cut in five equal pieces. How long is each piece? _____

34. A delivery truck has 1,250 gallons of heating oil at the beginning of the day. At the end of the day, it has 750.4 gallons. How many gallons were delivered?

_____

35. Silvio types 382 words in 8 minutes. Find how many words he types per minute. Round your answer to the nearest whole number. _____

36. **For Your Portfolio**   Get a stop watch. Time yourself doing a task, such as filling a glass with water and pouring it into a few smaller containers. Record your time. Repeat the task ten times and keep track of your results. On a separate piece of paper, write a paragraph describing how your time changed during the ten trials. Find and record the difference between your best and worst times.

Chapter 6   Practice Test

Compare. Use < or >.

1. 0.61 _____ 0.7

2. 1.23 _____ 1.045

3. 0.8 _____ 0.08

Write each fraction as a decimal.

4. $\frac{3}{8}$ = _____

5. $\frac{9}{20}$ = _____

6. $\frac{23}{25}$ = _____

7. $\frac{2}{9}$ = _____

Add or subtract.

8. $3.5 + 2.17$ = _____

9. $9.1 - 4.28$ = _____

10. $24.5 + 6.23$ = _____

11. $3.48 + 11.9$ = _____

12. $21.7 - 6.72$ = _____

13. $8.3 + 0.87$ = _____

Multiply or divide. Round any repeating decimal to the nearest hundredth.

14. 9.4×0.3 = _____

15. $6.2 \div 0.5$ = _____

16. 0.008×0.03 = _____

17. $3.1 \div 4$ = _____

18. $1.1 \div 0.36$ = _____

19. 0.72×1.45 = _____

Solve each equation.

20. $a + 0.82 = 1.4$

21. $8b = 3.4$

a =

b =

22. $x - 4.6 = 12$

23. $\frac{m}{9.4} = 15$

x =

m =

Solve.

24. In a 200-meter race, Hilary's time was 23.2 seconds and Judy's time was 24.14 seconds. How much faster was Hilary than Judy? _____

25. Mrs. Cohen paid $6.48 for 4.2 yards of ribbon. How much did she pay per yard? Round the answer to the nearest cent.

   _____

Chapter 7

Proportions and Percents

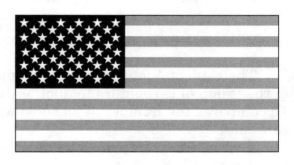

◢ OBJECTIVES:

In this chapter, you will learn

- *To write a ratio and a rate*
- *To identify and solve proportions*
- *To solve problems using proportions*
- *To write and use percents*
- *To solve a percent problem using a proportion or a decimal*

Ratio and proportion are important ideas in art and design.

In 1912, President William Howard Taft established federal regulations about the shape of the United States flag. The ratio of width to length for any official United States flag must be 1 to 1.9. That means for every 1 unit of width, the flag must be 1.9 units long.

Do these regulations mean that all flags must be the same size? Suppose you want to make a U.S. flag. How would you decide if the flag follows the regulations? What measurements would you take? How would you compare the measurements?

7•1 Understanding Ratio

To write a ratio and a rate

WORDS TO LEARN

Ratio *a comparison of two quantities*

Equivalent ratios *ratios that have the same value*

Rate *a special kind of ratio that compares quantities of two different units*

On a construction job, carpenters work in teams made up of both apprentices and journeymen. An apprentice is a person who is learning a skill or trade. A journeyman is an experienced, skilled worker. One company's policy states that the ratio of journeymen to apprentices must be 4:6 to help ensure the safety of new carpenters.

New Idea

A **ratio** (RAY-shoh) compares two quantities. The order of numbers in a ratio is important. Ratios can be written in three different ways— with the word "to," with a colon (:), or as a fraction. Ratios can compare quantities in different ways: part to part, part to whole, or whole to part. The order of the numbers in a ratio is very important.

Example: Express the ratio of journeymen to apprentices in three ways.

4 to 6, 4:6, and $\frac{4}{6}$

The ratio of 4 journeymen to 6 apprentices compares one part of the group of carpenters to another (part to part). The ratio of 4 to 10 compares the number of journeymen to the whole group (part to whole).

A ratio, like a fraction, can be simplified. **Equivalent ratios** (ee-KWIHV-uh-luhnt RAY-shohz) have the same value.

A **rate** (rayt) is a special kind of ratio that compares quantities in different units.

Examples: Simplify $\frac{4}{6}$ and write an equivalent ratio.

The ratio $\frac{4}{6}$ can be simplified as $\frac{2}{3}$.
The ratio 2:3 is equivalent to the ratio 4:6.

We can write a rate to describe a car traveling.

The speed of a car is a rate. A car can travel at a rate of $\frac{50 \text{ miles}}{1 \text{ hour}}$.

Sometimes a rate is not expressed in its simplest form. If a car travels 240 miles in 4 hours, its rate can be expressed as a ratio, $\frac{240 \text{ miles}}{4 \text{ hours}}$, which can be simplified to 60 miles per hour.

Focus on the Idea

A ratio is a comparison of two quantities. Equivalent ratios have the same value. Rates are special ratios that compare quantities of two different units.

Practice

Write each ratio as a fraction in simplest form. The first one is done for you.

1. 4 oranges to 1 glass of juice = _____ $\frac{4}{1}$ _____

2. 6 eggs to 4 omelettes = _____

3. 6 cups of water to 3 cups of rice = _____

4. 25 people to 5 minivans = _____

 Write each rate as an equivalent ratio with 1 as the denominator. The first one is done for you.

5. $\frac{210 \text{ miles}}{7 \text{ hours}} = \frac{30 \text{ mi}}{h}$

6. $\frac{600 \text{ feet}}{30 \text{ seconds}} = $ _____

7. $\frac{\$16}{2.5 \text{ pounds}} = $ _____

8. $\frac{\$25}{4 \text{ shirts}} = $ _____

9. $\frac{240 \text{ miles}}{12 \text{ gallons}} = $ _____

10. $\frac{\$5}{10 \text{ pens}} = $ _____

Apply the Idea

Write a ratio in simplest form for each description.

11. There are 12 juniors and 15 seniors on the swim team. What is the ratio of juniors to seniors? _____

12. Dave has 44 fiction books and 10 nonfiction books. What is the ratio of nonfiction books to all his books? _____

13. A baseball team has 9 new players out of a total of 25 players. What is the ratio of new players to total players? _____

Write About It

14. This is a pattern for tiles on a floor. Write a paragraph that describes how to find the number of tiles needed for each color. Use a ratio to explain the process.

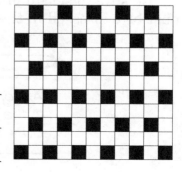

_____

_____

_____

7•2 Using Ratio and Proportion

IN THIS LESSON, YOU WILL LEARN
To identify a proportion using the cross-products rule

WORDS TO LEARN
Proportion *a statement that two ratios are equal*
Cross-products *in the proportion $\frac{a}{b} = \frac{c}{d}$ the cross-products are ad and bc*

Joe is planning a party. He wants to serve orange punch and has a recipe that says to mix seltzer and orange juice in a ratio of 1 part seltzer to 2 parts orange juice. How can Joe use this recipe for his party?

New Idea

A **proportion** (proh-PAWR-shuhn) is a statement that two ratios are equal. If $\frac{a}{b} = \frac{c}{d}$, *ad* and *bc* are the **cross-products** (kraws PRAHD-ukts). In any proportion, the cross-products are equal.

Example: Joe made orange punch using 1 quart of seltzer and 2 quarts of orange juice. When the punch was gone, Joe made more, using 2 quarts of seltzer and 4 quarts of orange juice. Is the ratio the same for each batch?

$$\frac{\text{seltzer}}{\text{orange juice}} = \frac{1 \text{ quart}}{2 \text{ quarts}} \quad \text{and} \quad \frac{\text{seltzer}}{\text{orange juice}} = \frac{2 \text{ quarts}}{4 \text{ quarts}}$$

Do the ratios form a proportion?

$$\frac{1}{2} \stackrel{?}{=} \frac{2}{4}$$

$$1 \cdot 4 \stackrel{?}{=} 2 \cdot 2 \quad \leftarrow \text{Multiply to find cross-products.}$$

$$4 = 4 \quad \leftarrow \text{Cross-products are equal.}$$

Yes, the two ratios form a proportion because their cross-products are equal.

Be sure to set up proportions correctly. The ratios in a proportion must be expressed in the same order.

Focus on the Idea
A proportion is a statement that two ratios are equal. In the proportion $\frac{a}{b} = \frac{c}{d}$ the cross-products are equal: ad = bc.

Practice

Is the statement a proportion? Write *yes* or *no*. Show your work. The first one is done for you.

1. $\frac{1}{2} \overset{?}{=} \frac{2}{3}$

   $1 \cdot 3 \overset{?}{=} 2 \cdot 2$

   $3 \overset{?}{=} 4$

   _____no_____

2. $\frac{3}{8} \overset{?}{=} \frac{6}{16}$

   _____

3. $\frac{4}{6} \overset{?}{=} \frac{8}{12}$

   _____

4. $\frac{6}{7} \overset{?}{=} \frac{8}{9}$

   _____

5. $\frac{10}{12} \overset{?}{=} \frac{15}{18}$

   _____

6. $\frac{11}{22} \overset{?}{=} \frac{15}{30}$

   _____

7. $\frac{4}{9} \overset{?}{=} \frac{9}{14}$

   _____

8. $\frac{5}{8} \overset{?}{=} \frac{7}{10}$

   _____

9. $\frac{8}{20} \overset{?}{=} \frac{12}{30}$

   _____

10. $\frac{30}{40} \overset{?}{=} \frac{21}{28}$

    _____

11. $\frac{\frac{1}{3}}{\frac{1}{2}} \overset{?}{=} \frac{2}{3}$

    _____

12. $\frac{2.5}{5} \overset{?}{=} \frac{4}{6}$

    _____

Apply the Idea

13. A recipe that makes 4 servings calls for 2 cups of rice. Jorge used 6 cups of rice to make enough of the recipe for 12 people. Show that Jorge's ratio of servings to rice is the same as in the recipe.

    _____

14. A camp advertises that it has three counselors for every ten children. During the last session, there were 18 counselors and 60 children. Show that the ratio of counselors to children is the same as the advertised ratio.

    _____

Write About It

15. In the United States House of Representatives, each state is assigned a number of representatives based on its total population. A state is allowed one representative for approximately 519,000 people. Write a paragraph explaining how a proportion is used here.

    _____

    _____

    _____

↘7•3 Solving Proportions

↘**IN THIS LESSON, YOU WILL LEARN**

To solve proportions using the cross-products rule

To solve problems using proportions

WORDS TO LEARN

Variable *a letter that stands for an unknown number*

Odetta is mixing paint. To get the color green she wants, she must mix 2 parts yellow with 3 parts blue. She has 1 quart of yellow paint. How much blue paint does she need?

New Idea

The cross-products rule can be used to find an unknown number in a proportion. Use a **variable** to represent the unknown number. (See Lesson 1•2.)

Example: How much blue paint does Odetta need?

Odetta wants to mix 2 parts of yellow paint with 3 parts of blue paint. Set up a proportion. Let x stand for the unknown number of quarts of blue paint.

$$\frac{2}{3} \qquad \leftarrow \text{ratio of yellow to blue}$$

$$\frac{2}{3} = \frac{1}{x} \qquad \leftarrow \text{proportion}$$

$$2 \cdot x = 3 \cdot 1 \qquad \leftarrow \text{cross-products}$$

$$2x = 3$$

$$\frac{2x}{2} = \frac{3}{2} \qquad \leftarrow \text{Divide both sides by 2.}$$

$$x = \frac{3}{2} \text{ or } 1\frac{1}{2} \quad \leftarrow \text{Simplify.}$$

Odetta needs $1\frac{1}{2}$ quarts of blue paint.

↘**Focus on the Idea**

To solve a proportion problem, set up a proportion using a variable for the unknown. Then use the cross-products rule to write an equation. Solve for the variable.

Practice

Solve for the variable. The first one is done for you.

1. $\frac{x}{9} = \frac{2}{3}$

   $3x = 18$

   $\frac{3x}{3} = \frac{18}{3}$

   $x = 6$

2. $\frac{a}{3} = \frac{5}{6}$

3. $\frac{11}{w} = \frac{88}{40}$

4. $\frac{10}{4} = \frac{25}{g}$

5. $\frac{4}{m} = \frac{22}{33}$

6. $\frac{8}{14} = \frac{50}{z}$

Apply the Idea

Write the letter of the correct proportion. Then solve the problem.

7. When Mr. Rodriguez orders milk for his store, the ratio of skim milk to whole milk is 2:5. He is ordering 50 quarts of skim milk. How much whole milk should he order?

   _____

   a. $\frac{2}{5} = \frac{x}{50}$

   b. $\frac{2}{5} = \frac{50}{x}$

   c. $\frac{2}{x} = \frac{50}{5}$

8. A recipe for granola calls for 3 parts raisins to 5 parts nuts. Tom has $2\frac{1}{2}$ pounds of nuts. How many pounds of raisins does he need? _____

   a. $\frac{3}{5} = \frac{2.5}{x}$

   b. $\frac{3}{x} = \frac{2.5}{5}$

   c. $\frac{3}{5} = \frac{x}{2.5}$

9. A copier can make 40 copies in 3 minutes. How long will it take to make 2,400 copies? _____

   a. $\frac{40}{3} = \frac{x}{2,400}$

   b. $\frac{40}{3} = \frac{2,400}{x}$

   c. $\frac{40}{x} = \frac{2,400}{3}$

Write About It

10. Explain how to change the following recipe to serve 8. Use another sheet of paper if you need more space.

    Chili (serves 4)

    1 pound ground beef　　　　1 onion

    $1\frac{1}{2}$ cups tomato sauce　　2 cups kidney beans

    2 teaspoons chili powder

    _____

    _____

▼**IN THIS LESSON, YOU WILL LEARN**

To write and use percents

To write a percent as a fraction or a decimal

To write a fraction or a decimal as a percent

WORDS TO LEARN

Percent *a ratio that compares a number to 100*

Stan and Luis play basketball for their high school team. Stan made 424 of 942 field goal attempts last season. Luis made 410 of his 975 attempts. Their records have more meaning when they are expressed as percents: Stan shot 45% and Luis shot 42%.

New Idea

The word percent means per hundred. A **percent** (puhr-SEHNT) is a ratio that compares a number to 100. The symbol % is used to show percent, but percents also can be written as fractions or decimals.

Example: Change Luis' and Stan's records to fraction and decimal form.

$$42\% = \frac{42}{100} \quad \leftarrow \text{Express as 42 hundredths.}$$
$$= 0.42$$

$$45\% = \frac{45}{100} \quad \leftarrow \text{Express as 45 hundredths.}$$
$$= 0.45$$

It can be useful to change a decimal or a fraction to a percent. You easily can change a decimal to a percent by moving the decimal point two places to the right and writing a % sign.

Example: Write each decimal as a percent. 0.32   0.015   3.5

$$0.32 = 32\% \quad 0.015 = 1.5\% \quad 3.50 = 350\%$$

To change a fraction to a percent, first change the fraction to a decimal. Then change the decimal to a percent.

Example: Write each fraction as a percent. $\frac{3}{4}$ $\frac{1}{3}$ $1\frac{1}{5}$

Fraction		Decimal		Percent
$\frac{3}{4}$	=	0.75	=	75%
$\frac{1}{3}$	=	$0.\overline{33}$	=	$33\frac{1}{3}\%$
$1\frac{1}{5}$	=	1.2	=	120%

Focus on the Idea

Percent is a ratio that means per one hundred. A percent can be written as a fraction or a decimal. A fraction or a decimal can be written as a percent.

Practice

 Write a percent for each fraction or decimal. The first one is done for you.

1. $\frac{3}{100}$ = ___3%___

2. 0.25 = _____

3. $\frac{71}{100}$ = _____

4. $\frac{7}{8}$ = _____

5. 0.21 = _____

6. 0.9 = _____

7. 1.02 = _____

8. 0.002 = _____

9. 1 = _____

10. 97 out of 100 = _____

11. $1\frac{3}{4}$ = _____

12. 5 = _____

Write each percent as a fraction and as a decimal. The first one is done for you.

		Fraction	Decimal
13.	15%	$\frac{15}{100} = \frac{3}{20}$	0.15
14.	45%		
15.	7%		
16.	125%		

Apply the Idea

Write a percent for each underlined word or phrase.

17. In a survey, <u>4 out of 100 people</u> said their favorite sport is rock climbing. _____

18. <u>Half</u> of the people who live in our building have lived here for more than 5 years. _____

19. A department store is offering $\frac{1}{4}$ off the regular price of sheets. _____

20. To find the sales tax, the clerk multiplies the cost of an item by <u>0.035</u>. _____

Write About It

21. Write a paragraph explaining what it means when the TV news reports that 80% of the registered voters participated in an election.

_____

_____

7•5 Using Proportions with Percents

◀ **IN THIS LESSON, YOU WILL LEARN**

To write a proportion for a percent problem

WORDS TO LEARN

Actuary *a person who uses mathematics and statistics to make predictions for insurance companies*

Maria is an actuary for the Good Health Insurance Company. As an **actuary** (AK-choo-ehr-ee), she uses mathematics and statistics to make predictions. Part of her job is to use accident records to estimate what to charge people for their car insurance. She gathers information on the ages of people who have had car accidents. She then can predict the number of people in various age groups who might have accidents in the future.

New Idea

Writing a proportion and using the cross-products rule is one way of solving many percent problems. Any percent can be written as a ratio of part to whole. Because a percent is a ratio comparing a number to 100, we can write a proportion using two equivalent ratios.

$$\frac{\text{part}}{\text{whole}} = \frac{\%}{100}$$

Example: Maria found that 22 out of 88 people between the ages of 20 and 25 have had accidents. What percent is the ratio 22 out of 88?

$$\frac{22}{88} \begin{array}{l} \leftarrow \text{part} \\ \leftarrow \text{whole} \end{array}$$

Let x equal the missing percent. Then write the proportion $\frac{22}{88} = \frac{x}{100}$ with x representing the missing value.

◀ **Focus on the Idea**

To solve problems involving percents and proportions, identify the numbers that represent parts of the whole, and the numbers that represent the whole. Then write a proportion using a variable for the missing number.

Practice

Write a proportion. Do not solve. The first one is done for you.

1. 225 is what percent of 300? $\dfrac{225}{300} = \dfrac{x}{100}$

2. 40 out of 50 is what percent? _____

3. 97.5 out of 150 is what percent? _____

4. 55 is what percent of 35? _____

Extend the Idea

If you know the percent, you can use a proportion to find either the part or the whole.

Examples: Maria must predict: If 25% of people between the ages of 20 and 25 have accidents, how many of the 600 people with Good Health Insurance in this age group will probably have accidents?

You can write a proportion using this information.

$$\text{part} \rightarrow \dfrac{x}{600} = \dfrac{25}{100} \leftarrow \text{percent} \atop \text{whole} \rightarrow$$

✓Check the Math

5. Thuan and Quentin had lunch at a restaurant. They left a tip of $3.25, which was 15% of the bill. Can you find the total bill by using the proportion $\dfrac{\$3.25}{x} = \dfrac{15}{100}$? _____

Practice

Write a proportion using *x* for the unknown number. Do not solve. The first one is done for you.

6. 8 is 20% of what number? $\dfrac{8}{x} = \dfrac{20}{100}$

7. What number is 30% of 90? _____

8. Six is 12% of what number? _____

9. What number is 45% of 200? _____

Apply the Idea

Write a proportion for each problem. Do not solve.

10. Ms. Williams paid $32, which was 20% of her doctor's bill. How much was the doctor's bill? _____

✏ Write About It

11. How do you think actuaries use information from the past to predict what might happen in the future?

_____

◣7●6 Solving Percent Problems

▸ **IN THIS LESSON, YOU WILL LEARN**

To solve a percent problem using a proportion

To solve a percent problem using a decimal

WORDS TO LEARN

Meteorology *the science of observing and predicting weather*

Meteorology (meet-ee-uhr-AHL-uh-jee) is the science of observing and predicting weather. Many meteorologists use records and equations to predict weather patterns. Although modern equipment has improved meteorologists' accuracy, their predictions are not perfect.

New Idea

You can solve any percent problem by writing a proportion and then using the cross-products rule.

Example: In the last five years, it rained 20 days out of 30 in April. What was the percent of rainy days?

The 20 is part of the 30 days of the month.

$$\frac{20}{30} = \frac{x}{100} \quad \leftarrow \text{proportion}$$

$$20 \cdot 100 = 30 \cdot x \quad \leftarrow \text{Find cross-products.}$$

$$\frac{2{,}000}{30} = \frac{30x}{30} \quad \leftarrow \text{Divide both sides by 30.}$$

$$66.7\% = x \quad \leftarrow \text{rounded to the nearest tenth}$$

The percent of rainy days was 66.7%.

You also can solve some percent problems by changing the percent to a decimal and multiplying.

Example: Solve by changing the percent to a decimal.

Rita gets a 10% discount on everything she buys in the store where she works. How much will she pay for a pair of $65 shoes?

Change 10% to a decimal. 10% = 0.10
Multiply the original price by 0.10.
$65.00 \cdot 0.10 = $6.50

Rita will pay $6.50 less than $65, or $65 − $6.50, which is $58.50.

Focus on the Idea

Percent problems can be solved by writing a proportion and using the cross-products rule or by changing the percent to a decimal and multiplying.

Practice

Write and solve a proportion for each question. Round your answers to the nearest tenth, if necessary. The first one is done for you.

1. 25 is what percent of 300?

$$\frac{25}{300} = \frac{x}{100}$$
$$2,500 = 300x$$
$$\frac{2,500}{300} = \frac{300x}{300}$$
$$8.3\% = x$$

2. 8 is 20% of what number?

3. What is 30% of 90?

4. 40 out of 50 is what percent?

Apply the Idea

Write a proportion or use a decimal to solve each exercise.

5. A survey reported that 62% of the town residents support the mayor. The town has 17,500 residents. How many residents support the mayor? _____

6. If 234 grams of ore produce 36 grams of copper, what percent of copper does the ore contain? Round to the nearest tenth of a percent. _____

7. A sales representative's commission is 3% of the total of her sales. How much commission will she earn if she sells a car for $15,000? _____

Write About It

8. Write a few sentences using some of the following words: *often, never, sometimes, always, seldom, usually, once in a while, rarely.* Then rewrite each sentence, using a percent instead of the word in the list.

_____

_____

Chapter 7   Review

In This Chapter, You Have Learned
- To write a ratio
- To write a rate
- To identify a proportion using the cross-products rule
- To solve proportions using the cross-products rule
- To solve problems using proportions
- To write and use percents
- To write a percent as a fraction or a decimal, and to write a fraction or a decimal as a percent
- To write a proportion for a percent problem
- To solve a percent problem using a proportion
- To solve a percent problem using a decimal

Words You Know
From the lists of "Words to Learn," choose the word or phrase that best completes each statement.

1. The _____ of vowels to consonants in the word "MISSISSIPPI" is 4:7.
2. A(n) _____ is a comparison of two different units of measurement.
3. The ratios $\frac{2}{3}$ and $\frac{4}{6}$ are _____ .
4. A(n) _____ is a statement that two ratios are equal.
5. In a proportion, the _____ are equal.
6. A(n) _____ is a ratio that compares a number to 100.

More Practice
Write each ratio as a fraction in simplest form.

7. 2 eggs to 4 cups of flour _____
8. 5 oranges to 3 apples _____
9. 6 adults to 5 children _____
10. 4 magazines to 12 books _____

Simplify each rate so that the denominator shows a quantity of 1.

11. $\frac{250 \text{ miles}}{5 \text{ hours}}$ _____   12. $\frac{64 \text{ ounces of juice}}{8 \text{ servings}}$ _____

Is each statement a proportion? Write *yes* or *no*.

13. $\frac{3}{10} \overset{?}{=} \frac{6}{20}$ _____   14. $\frac{5}{6} \overset{?}{=} \frac{11}{12}$ _____

Solve each proportion.

15. $\frac{x}{6} = \frac{7}{2}$ _____

16. $\frac{3}{5} = \frac{x}{15}$ _____

17. $\frac{4}{x} = \frac{10}{11}$ _____

18. $\frac{6}{9} = \frac{4}{x}$ _____

Write each as a percent.

19. 6 out of 100 = _____

20. $\frac{1}{2}$ = _____

21. 0.6 = _____

22. 1.8 = _____

23. $\frac{4}{5}$ = _____

24. 0.02 = _____

Write and solve a proportion for each problem.

25. What percent of 60 is 3? _____

26. Find 15% of 200. _____

27. Five is 2% of what number? _____

28. What is 6% of $140? _____

Problems You Can Solve

29. A recipe for 15 pancakes uses 2 eggs. How many eggs are needed for 60 pancakes? _____

30. Judy's car traveled 350 miles on 14 gallons of gasoline. How many miles per gallon did the car get? _____

31. The sales tax in New View Township is 5%. What is the amount of sales tax that must be paid on a radio that costs $35? _____

32. A scale drawing uses the ratio 1 centimeter to 3 meters. On the drawing, a wall is 4 centimeters long. How long is the actual wall? _____

33. A doctor says that no more than 15% of our daily calories should come from fat. How many calories from fat are permitted on a 2,000-calories-per-day diet? _____

34. **For Your Portfolio**   Cut out advertisements from newspapers for discount sales. Make up four problems based on those advertisements.

_____

_____

_____

_____

_____

Chapter 7   Practice Test

Write each ratio as a fraction in simplest form.

1. 4 hens to 22 eggs _____

2. 9 children to 2 day-care workers _____

Write each ratio as a rate with a denominator of 1.

3. 2,400 copies in 3 minutes _____

4. $13 for 4 pounds _____

Is each statement a proportion? Write *yes* or *no*.

5. $\frac{1}{2} \stackrel{?}{=} \frac{3}{4}$ _____

6. $\frac{2}{5} \stackrel{?}{=} \frac{24}{60}$ _____

7. $\frac{3}{10} \stackrel{?}{=} \frac{60}{200}$ _____

Solve each proportion.

8. $\frac{x}{3} = \frac{12}{2}$

9. $\frac{10}{7} = \frac{14}{x}$

10. $\frac{5}{8} = \frac{x}{22}$

Write each as a percent.

11. 3 out of 5 = _____

12. $\frac{5}{8}$ = _____

13. 0.7 = _____

Write each percent as a fraction and as a decimal.

	Fraction	Decimal
14. 40%	_____	_____
15. 3%	_____	_____
16. 250%	_____	_____

Solve.

17. A recipe for soup calls for 4 cups of broth and 3 cups of vegetables. How many cups of vegetables will be needed for 12 cups of broth? _____

18. A quality control inspector found that 3 out of 120 light bulbs were defective. What percent was defective? _____

19. A washing machine costs $270. It is on sale this week for 20% off the cost. How much will be saved buying it this week? _____

20. Mr. Grant paid $25 for an outpatient procedure at a hospital. This was 20% of the total fee. What was the total fee?

_____

Chapter 8

Graphing Equations

OBJECTIVES:

In this chapter, you will learn

- *To graph the solution of an equation on a number line*
- *To locate points on a coordinate plane*
- *To identify coordinates of points on a coordinate plane*
- *To find ordered-pair solutions to equations with two variables*
- *To graph the solutions to an equation with two variables*

Firefighters need many skills. Among these are the ability to read maps and determine locations. One examination for firefighters includes the following exercise.

A fire truck is heading north on Ryder Street between Third and Second streets. The driver receives a call to go to a burning building at Allerton and First streets. The map shows that Allerton and Ryder streets are one way going north. Main Street is one way going south. Market Street is one way going northwest. First and Third streets are one way going east, and Second Street is one way going west. Find the location of the fire truck when it received the call. Draw on the map the shortest route the fire truck should take to the fire without going the wrong way on any one-way streets.

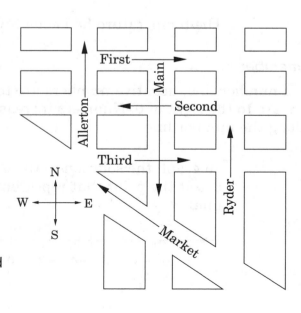

▼8•1 Graphing Equations on a Number Line

Between 6 P.M. and 10 P.M., the temperature dropped 12°C. The temperature at 10 P.M. was −4°C. What had been the temperature at 6 P.M.?

New Idea

You can use an equation to solve many kinds of problems. Sometimes a picture can help you understand the solution of an equation. You can **graph a solution** (graf uh suh-LOO-shuhn) to an equation by using a number line to show the solution.

Example: What was the temperature at 6 P.M.? Write an equation. Let t represent the temperature at 6 P.M.

$$t - 12 = -4 \qquad \leftarrow \text{equation}$$

$$t - 12 + 12 = -4 + 12 \qquad \leftarrow \text{Add 12 to both sides of the equation.}$$

$$t = 8 \qquad \leftarrow \text{Simplify.}$$

The temperature had been 8°C at 6 P.M.

⤸Remember

On a number line, negative numbers are to the left of 0. Positive numbers are to the right of 0. Numbers increase in value from left to right along the number line.

To graph the solution to the equation above, draw a dot at the point that represents 8 on the number line.

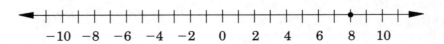

Focus on the Idea

When you solve an equation, you get a value for the variable. You can graph the solution to the equation on a number line using a dot to represent the solution.

Practice

Solve the equation. Then label a number line and graph the solution to the equation. The first two are done for you.

1. $x + 2 = -4$

$x + 2 - 2 = -4 - 2$

$x = -4 + (-2)$

$x = \underline{\quad -6 \quad}$

$-8 \quad -6 \quad -4 \quad -2 \quad 0 \quad 2 \quad 4$

2. $\frac{h}{2} = -1$

$2(\frac{h}{2}) = 2(-1)$

$h = \underline{\quad -2 \quad}$

$-8 \quad -6 \quad -4 \quad -2 \quad 0 \quad 2 \quad 4$

3. $4l = -3$

$l = \underline{\hspace{3cm}}$

4. $y - 4 = 1\frac{1}{2}$

$y = \underline{\hspace{3cm}}$

5. $m - 0.6 = -0.4$

$m = \underline{\hspace{3cm}}$

6. $-0.2f = 0.8$

$f = \underline{\hspace{3cm}}$

Apply the Idea

Write an equation for each problem. Solve the equation. Then, in the margin, draw a number line and graph the solution.

7. At the end of the day, there were 3 quarts of juice at the day-care center. During the day, 2 quarts of juice had been served. How many quarts of juice had there been at the beginning of the day? $\underline{\hspace{2cm}}$

8. Five notebooks cost $3.20. What is the cost of one notebook? $\underline{\hspace{2cm}}$

9. Gwen sawed a board into three equal pieces. Each piece was $\frac{3}{4}$ foot long. How long had the board been? $\underline{\hspace{2cm}}$

✎ Write About It

10. Think of some number lines that are vertical, rather than horizontal. Where are the positive numbers? Where are the negative numbers? Explain your answers.

$\underline{\hspace{12cm}}$

▶ **IN THIS LESSON, YOU WILL LEARN**

To locate points on a coordinate plane

To identify coordinates of points on a coordinate plane

WORDS TO LEARN

Coordinate plane *a flat region formed by two perpendicular number lines*

***x*-axis** *the horizontal number line on a coordinate plane*

***y*-axis** *the vertical number line on a coordinate plane*

Coordinate *a number that locates a position along a number line*

Origin *the point at which the x-axis and the y-axis meet*

Ordered pair *two numbers that name the x-coordinate and the y-coordinate of a point*

Raúl can't find Greenwich Village on the map. Becky stops and shows Raúl the index of locations on the map. It states that Greenwich Village is located at B2. How will this help Raúl find Greenwich Village on the map?

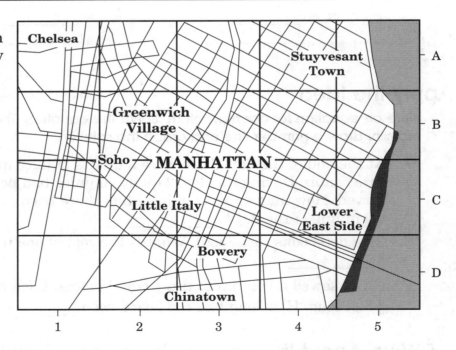

New Idea

A **coordinate plane** (kuh-AWR-duh-niht playn) is a flat region formed by two perpendicular number lines. The horizontal number line is called the ***x*-axis** (EHKS-ak-sihs). The vertical number line is called the ***y*-axis** (WY-ak-sihs). Each point along the number line is called a **coordinate**. The point at which the two axes meet is called the **origin** (AWR-uh-jihn).

Every point on the coordinate plane at the right can be located by a pair of numbers. The **ordered pair** (AWR-duhrd pair) for a point is made up of the two numbers that name the *x*-coordinate and the *y*-coordinate for that point. The order of the numbers—*x*-coordinate, then *y*-coordinate—is important. The ordered pair for the origin is (0, 0).

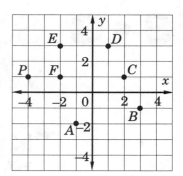

Example: What is the ordered pair for point *P*?

Point *P* is located four units to the left of the origin and one unit up. The ordered pair for point *P* is (−4, 1).

Focus on the Idea

Any points on a coordinate plane can be located by an ordered pair of numbers. In an ordered pair, the first number names the coordinate along the x-axis. The second number names the coordinate along the y-axis.

Practice

Name the ordered pair for each lettered point on the coordinate plane above. The first one is done for you.

1. *A* ___(−1, −2)___
2. *B* _____
3. *C* _____
4. *D* _____
5. *E* _____
6. *F* _____

On the coordinate plane to the right, graph and label the lettered point for each ordered pair.

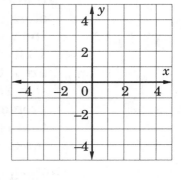

7. *I* at (2, 3)
8. *J* at (−1, 0)
9. *K* at (2, −2)
10. *L* at (−3, −2)
11. *M* at (−1, −2)
12. *N* at (0, 3)

Apply the Idea

13. Write at least five ordered pairs that could be graphed as points on a coordinate plane and then connected to form the following:

    a. a capital letter L _____

    b. the first letter of your name _____

Write About It

14. Explain how the map on page 134 is like a coordinate plane.

    _____

    _____

➤8•3 Solving Equations with Two Variables

IN THIS LESSON, YOU WILL LEARN

To find ordered-pair solutions for equations with two variables

WORDS TO LEARN

Equation with two variables an equation that expresses the relationship between two quantities

Elvira wants to use 12 feet of fencing to enclose a rectangular storage area for her lawn-care equipment. There are many possible combinations of length and width that she could use to make her fence.

New Idea

Sometimes there are two quantities in a problem. You can use two different variables to represent the two quantities. The relationship between the quantities can be written as an **equation with two variables** (ih-KWAY-shuhn wihth too VAIR-ee-uh-buhls).

Example: Use an equation with two variables to find the possible measurements for Elvira's storage area. Use ℓ for the length and w for the width. The total amount of fencing, 12 feet, represents the perimeter of the storage area. Using the perimeter formula, $P = 2\ell + 2w$, an equation for this problem is $2\ell + 2w = 12$. You can make a table that shows pairs of values for ℓ and w that make this equation true.

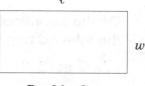

$P = 2\ell + 2w$

Each pair of values that makes the equation true can be written as an ordered pair (ℓ, w). The ordered pairs are solutions to $2\ell + 2w = 12$.

$(1, 5), (2, 4), (3, 3), (4, 2), (5, 1)$

ℓ	w	$2\ell + 2w$
1	5	2(1) + 2(5) 12
2	4	2(2) + 2(4) 12
3	3	2(3) + 2(3) 12
4	2	2(4) + 2(2) 12
5	1	2(5) + 2(1) 12

Focus on the Idea

If an equation has two variables, it has many solutions. Each solution is an ordered pair. You can show the ordered-pair solutions in a table.

Practice

Complete the table of values for each equation. The first one is done for you.

1. For $y = x + 1$:

x	$y = x + 1$	(x, y)
1	$1 + 1 = 2$	$(1, 2)$
2	$2 + 1 = 3$	$(2, 3)$
3	$3 + 1 = 4$	$(3, 4)$

2. For $y = 2x$:

x	$y = 2x$	(x, y)
1		$(\ ,\ )$
2		$(\ ,\ )$
3		$(\ ,\ )$

3. For $y = 5 - x$:

x	$y = 5 - x$	(x, y)
1		$(\ ,\ )$
2		$(\ ,\ )$
3		$(\ ,\ )$

4. For $y = 2x - 5$:

x	$y = 2x - 5$	(x, y)
1		$(\ ,\ )$
2		$(\ ,\ )$
3		$(\ ,\ )$

Apply the Idea

5. Sam charges $2 to pick up a package, then $1 per mile to deliver it. An equation that shows how the total cost, y, changes with the number of miles, x, is $y = 2 + x$. Complete this table to find the total cost for deliveries of 1, 4, 10, and 25 miles.

x	$y = 2 + x$	*(miles, cost)*
1		
4		
10		
25		

Write About It

6. Refer to the example of Elvira's storage area. The ordered pairs $(0, 6)$ and $(6, 0)$ are solutions. Do these two solutions make sense? Explain.

_____

_____

_____

8•4 Graphing an Equation with Two Variables

IN THIS LESSON, YOU WILL LEARN

To graph the solutions to an equation with two variables

WORDS TO LEARN

Graph of an equation *the set of all points that are solutions to an equation*

Mr. Chang owns a fruit-and-nut store. He wants to make some signs that show the total cost for different amounts of fruits and nuts. Walnuts sell for $3 per pound. How can Mr. Chang list the prices for different amounts of walnuts?

New Idea

You can use a graph to show the relationship between two quantities, represented by variables. If an equation has two variables, the ordered pairs that are solutions to the equation can be located on a coordinate plane. The **graph of an equation** (graf uhv an ih-KWAY-shun) is the set of all points that are solutions to an equation.

Example: Draw a graph to show the relationship between each amount of walnuts and price.

If x stands for the number of pounds of walnuts, then $y = 3x$ is an equation for the price (y). Start with a table to find some of the ordered pairs that are solutions to the equation $y = 3x$. Then plot those points on a coordinate plane.

x	$y = 3x$	(x, y)
0	0	(0, 0)
1	3	(1, 3)
2	6	(2, 6)
3	9	(3, 9)

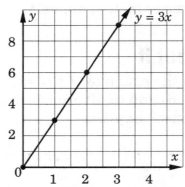

When the ordered pairs are graphed, they lie in a straight line. The line drawn through the points is the graph of the equation. Every point on that line is a solution to $y = 3x$.

Focus on the Idea

To draw the graph of an equation with two variables, first find ordered pairs that are solutions to the equation. Then locate the points on a coordinate plane. Draw a line through the points to graph the equation.

Practice

Complete each table to find the ordered pairs. Then graph each equation on a coordinate plane. The first one is done for you.

1. $y = 2x - 1$

x	y	(x, y)
0	−1	(0, −1)
1	1	(1, 1)
2	3	(2, 3)

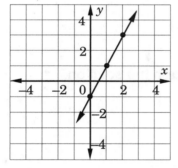

2. $y = 2 - 3x$

x	y	(x, y)
−1		
0		
1		

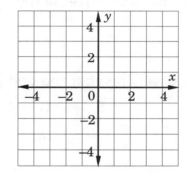

3. $y = \frac{x}{2} + 3$

x	y	(x, y)
0		
2		
4		

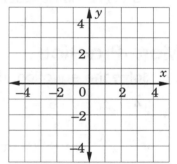

Apply the Idea

Al's Music Store is having a 25%–off sale. This means that the sale price (*y*) of every item in the store is equal to 75% of the regular price (*x*). The graph of *y* = 0.75*x* is shown at the right.

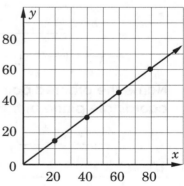

4. Find the sale price of a snare drum that regularly costs $80. _____

5. Find the regular price of a tambourine on sale for $30. _____

✎ Write About It

6. On a separate sheet of paper, write a paragraph that explains how the graph of an equation can be used to find solutions to the equation.

Chapter 8   Review

In This Chapter, You Have Learned
- To graph the solution of an equation on a number line
- To locate points on a coordinate plane
- To identify coordinates of points on a coordinate plane
- To find ordered-pair solutions to equations with two variables
- To graph the solutions to an equation with two variables

Words You Know

From the lists of "Words to Learn," choose the word or phrase that best completes each statement.

1. Any point on the coordinate plane can be located with a(n) _____, which has an x-coordinate and a y-coordinate.

2. The _____ is the horizontal number line, and the _____ is the vertical number line.

3. The point where the two axes meet is the _____.

More Practice

Solve the equation. Then label a number line and graph the solution.

4. $2x = -6$

$x =$ _____

5. $y - 3 = -1$

$y =$ _____

6. $h + 5 = 4$

$h =$ _____

7. $\frac{z}{3} = 1$

$z =$ _____

Name the ordered pair for each lettered point on the coordinate plane at the right.

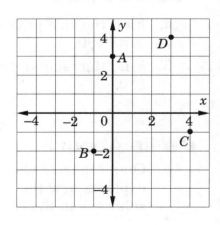

8. A _____

9. B _____

10. C _____

11. D _____

Graph and label the lettered point for each ordered pair on the coordinate plane at the right.

12. M at $(1, 4)$

13. N at $(0, -3)$

14. Q at $(-3, 2)$

15. P at $(-3, -4)$

Complete the table of values for each equation and graph on the coordinate plane.

16. $y = x + 3$

x	y	(x, y)
0		
1		
2		

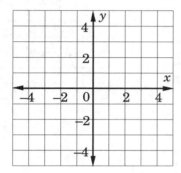

17. $y = 2x - 1$

x	y	(x, y)
0		
1		
2		

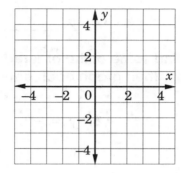

18. $y = -4x$

x	y	(x, y)
−1		
0		
1		

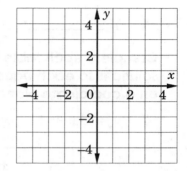

Problems You Can Solve

19. Joe had $650 in a savings account. He began to withdraw $50 per month to pay his health club dues. The equation for the amount of money in Joe's savings account (y) after x months of withdrawing $50 for dues is $y = 650 - 50x$.

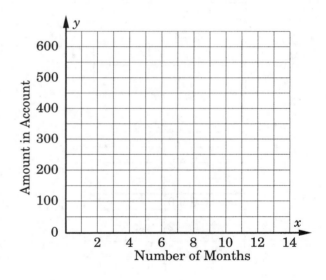

a. Sketch a graph of the equation on the coordinate plane at the right.

b. How much will be in Joe's savings account after he pays his dues for 3 months? _____

c. How many months will it take until Joe has no money left in his savings account? _____

20. For Your Portfolio Make a coordinate map for a section of your neighborhood. Locate the origin at a familiar place, such as the intersection of two main streets. The coordinates along the horizontal and vertical axes should represent blocks in each direction (north, south, east, and west). Explain how your map works and give ordered pairs for the location of three different places on the map that you visit often.

Chapter 8   Practice Test

Solve the equation. Graph the solution on a number line.

1. $3x = -6$

$x =$ _____

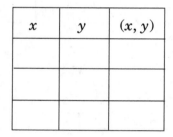

2. $x - 4 = -2$

$x =$ _____

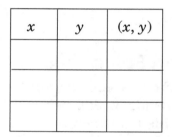

Name the ordered pair that represents each point on this coordinate plane.

3. W _____

4. X _____

5. Y _____

6. Z _____

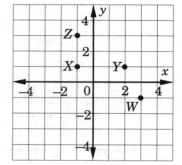

Complete each table to find some of the ordered-pair solutions to each equation. Then graph each equation on a coordinate plane.

7. $y = -x + 1$

x	y	(x, y)

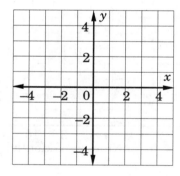

8. $y = -2x$

x	y	(x, y)

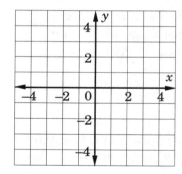

The equation for the weight in ounces (y) of x pounds is $y = 16x$. Use this information for exercises 9 and 10.

9. Find three ordered-pair solutions. Then graph the equation on the coordinate plane at the right. Consider using a scale where each line is more than one unit. Mark your scale on the graph. _____

10. Use the pattern you found in exercise 9 to find the number of ounces in 5.5 pounds. _____

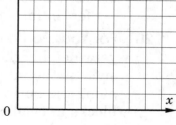

Chapter 9

Probability and Statistics

OBJECTIVES:

In this chapter, you will learn

- *To organize data into frequency tables and histograms*
- *To read graphs and use them to solve problems*
- *To read and interpret information from bar, line, and circle graphs*
- *To find the mean, median, and mode of a set of data*
- *To find the probability of a simple event*
- *To find an experimental probability*

Newspapers and magazines often report on the top money-making films of a week, month, or year. But, just because more movie-goers see one film rather than another does not mean that their choice of movies would be the same as *your* choice.

Take a survey of your friends and relatives. Ask questions like these:

How many times a year do you go to the movies?

What is the best movie you have seen this year?

What is your favorite movie of all time?

Predict some of the most popular answers. After you have taken your survey, look back at your predictions. How good were they? How can you describe your results?

9•1 Gathering and Recording Data

IN THIS LESSON, YOU WILL LEARN

To organize data into frequency tables and histograms

WORDS TO LEARN

Frequency table *a table that shows how often a certain data value occurs*

Histogram *a graph of the data in a frequency table*

Ms. Diaz works in a video rental store. She recorded the number of videos rented by 20 customers by writing the following:
1, 2, 2, 3, 2, 2, 1, 1, 1, 1, 2, 4, 2, 1, 1, 1, 3, 2, 1, 3

New Idea

Data should be organized so that they are easy to understand. One way to organize data is with a **frequency table** (FREE-kwuhn-see TAY-buhl), which tells the number of times each data value occurs. A second way is with a histogram. A **histogram** (HIS-toh-gram) is a graph of the data in a frequency table.

Example: Make a frequency table for Ms. Diaz's data.

Videos Rented	Number of Customers	Videos Rented	Number of Customers
1	9	3	3
2	7	4	1

A music store had the following ten sales in an hour.
$12.50, $34.21, $21.34, $63.21, $16.23, $29.34, $37.80, $112.43, $52.31, $16.95

Make a frequency table and a histogram for the music store sales data. In a frequency table, intervals of about $20 are a good choice for these data.

Amount of Sale	Number of Customers	Amount of Sale	Number of Customers
$0–$19.99	3	$60–$79.99	1
$20–$39.99	4	$80–$99.99	0
$40–$59.99	1	$100–$119.99	1

Look at the heights of the bars in the histogram to help you compare the different frequencies. You can quickly see which intervals had the greatest number of sales and which had the least.

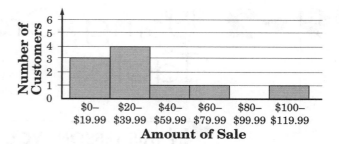

Focus on the Idea

Data can be organized into a frequency table or a histogram.

Practice

Arrange the data into a frequency table. Then make a histogram for the data. The first one has been started for you.

1. Number of sit-ups for each of 15 students:
   25, 14, 26, 35, 42, 15, 17, 24, 45, 38, 29, 11, 53, 70, 28.

Sit-ups	Students	Sit-ups	Students
0–9	*O*	40–49	_____
10–19	*4*	50–59	_____
20–29	_____	60–69	_____
30–39	_____	70–79	_____

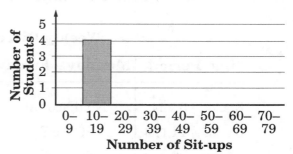

Apply the Idea

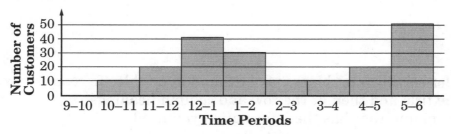

2. The histogram above shows the number of customers who visited a bookstore during each hour last Monday.

   a. How many customers visited the bookstore last Monday?

   _____

   b. What were the two busiest time periods? _____

✏ Write About It

3. Describe how you could use a frequency table or a histogram to organize the results of your movie survey on page 143.

   _____

   _____

⬥9•2 Using Graphs and Tables

◤ IN THIS LESSON, YOU WILL LEARN

To read graphs and use them to solve problems

WORDS TO LEARN

Discount *an amount by which the regular cost is reduced*

Many telephone companies offer a **discount** (DIHS-cownt) for calls made during evenings and weekends. A discount is the amount by which the regular cost of a call is reduced. The following discounts are available from The Friendly Phone Company.

Weekly Discounts

Time Period	Monday – Friday	Saturday	Sunday
8 A.M. – 5 P.M.	No discount	60% off	60% off
5 P.M. – 11 P.M.	30% off	60% off	30% off
11 P.M. – 8 A.M.	60% off	60% off	60% off

New Idea

Information for solving a problem may be found in a table. To read a table, look at the title and then at the row and column headings. Find the row and column that has the information you need.

Examples: What is the discount for a call made on Friday at 3 P.M.?

Find where the first row and the Monday–Friday column meet. There is no discount at 3 P.M. on Friday.

The regular cost of a call Sunday at 8 P.M. is $14.50. What is the discounted cost?

There is a 30% discount on Sunday at 8 P.M.

$14.50 × 0.30 = $4.35   ← Find 30% of $14.50

$14.50 − $4.35 = $10.15 ← Subtract from $14.50

The call would cost $10.15 on Sunday at 8:00 P.M.

Focus on the Idea

You can get information from a table by finding the row and column you need. Then look for the data in the table where that row and column meet.

Practice

Use this table to answer exercises 1 to 3. The first one is done for you.

Livestock on U.S. Farms (in Thousands)

Livestock	1994	1993	1992	1991	1990
Cattle	101,749	100,892	100,110	99,436	98,162
Dairy Cows	9,638	9,844	9,904	10,159	10,153
Sheep	9,079	10,191	10,850	11,200	11,363
Swine	55,630	58,340	56,974	52,360	51,150

1. In 1994, how many more dairy cows than sheep were there?

   9,638,000 − 9,079,000 = 559,000 more dairy cows than sheep

2. How many more cattle were there in 1994 than in 1990?

3. In 1993, what was the total number of sheep and swine?

Apply the Idea

Mrs. Wong is the director of a fitness club. Use this schedule of fees for the club to answer exercises 4 to 6.

Membership	1 year	18 months	2 years
Single	$350	$500	$650
Family	$500	$725	$900
Senior Citizen	$150	$200	$250

4. What is the cost of a family membership for 18 months?

5. What is the monthly cost of a 1-year membership for a senior citizen? _____

6. How much will Mr. and Mrs. Walsh save if they sign up for one 1-year family membership instead of two 1-year single memberships? _____

Write About It

7. Describe some ways you might use to be sure of reading the correct entry in a table.

⤴9•3 Using Bar, Line, and Circle Graphs

⤴ IN THIS LESSON, YOU WILL LEARN
To read and interpret information from bar, line, and circle graphs

WORDS TO LEARN
Bar graph *a graph that records and compares data, using bars*

Line graph *a graph that records changes in data, with plotted points connected by straight lines*

Circle graph *a graph that shows the relationship of parts of data to the whole*

Graphs are a good way to give a visual representation of information. Different kinds of graphs display different information. A bar graph appears on Mrs. Chee's electrical bill. It shows her monthly usage of electricity.

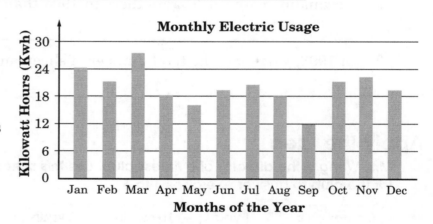

New Idea

A **bar graph** (bahr graf) compares data by using bars. The bars may be horizontal or vertical.

Example: In what month did Mrs. Chee use the least amount of electricity?

The bars on the electric company's graph are vertical. Notice that the vertical scale starts at 0. It is marked in increments of 6 kilowatt hours (Kwh). Read the graph by comparing the height of the bar for each month to the vertical scale.

You will see that September was the month in which Mrs. Chee used the least amount of electricity. You can estimate the number of kilowatt hours Mrs. Chee used in September, by reading across to the vertical scale. She used about 12 kilowatt hours of electricity in September.

Sometimes you need to see how data changes. A **line graph** (leyen graf) records changes in data with plotted points. Because the points are connected, it is easy to see where there is a pattern of increase or decrease.

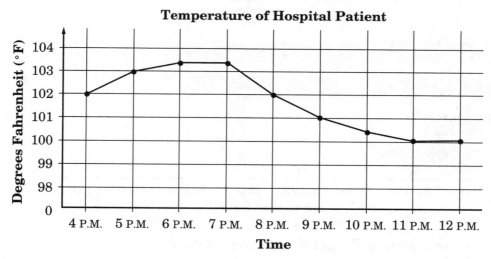

Temperature of Hospital Patient

Examples: What does the line graph above show about the patient's temperature?

The graph shows a hospital patient's temperature over an 8-hour period. The graph shows that the patient's temperature began to drop at 7 P.M.

What was the patient's temperature at 5 P.M.?

The patient's temperature at 5 P.M. is found by looking at the vertical scale. The temperature at 5 P.M was 103°F.

✓Check Your Understanding

1. Look at bar graph on page 148. During which three months did Mrs. Chee have the highest electrical usage? Explain why you think these months were high.

_____

_____

_____

◤Focus on the Idea

Different kinds of graphs serve different purposes. Bar graphs help to compare data. Line graphs show how data change.

_____

Practice

Use this bar graph to answer exercises 2 and 3.

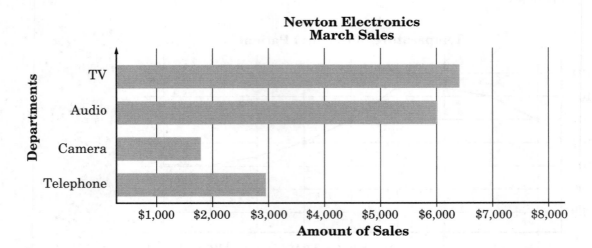

Newton Electronics March Sales

2. About how much were TV sales in March at Newton Electronics? _____

3. About how much more were audio sales than telephone sales in March? _____

Extend the Idea

A **circle graph** (SER-kuhl graf) shows the relationship of parts of data to the whole. The entire circle represents the whole, or 100%.

Example: This graph shows how the Maloney family spends its money each month. What part of their money do the Maloneys spend on their mortgage?

The graph shows that their mortgage payment is thirty percent (30%) of the family's total expenses.

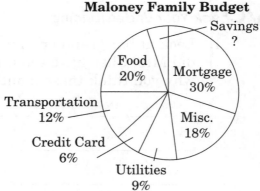

Maloney Family Budget

✓ *Check the Math*

4. Look at the circle graph. The Maloney family says they are saving 10% of their income. Is this correct? Explain your answer.

_____

_____

_____

5. What percent of Newton Electronics'
advertising budget will be spent on TV and
radio advertising together? _____

6. If the total advertising budget is $100,000, how
much will be spent on newspaper advertising?

_____

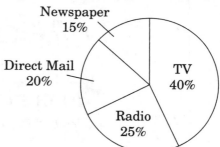

**Newton Electronics
Advertising Budget**

Newspaper 15%
Direct Mail 20%
TV 40%
Radio 25%

Apply the Idea

A traffic safety expert prepared this graph to show the
number of cars passing through a certain intersection
during a 13-hour period.

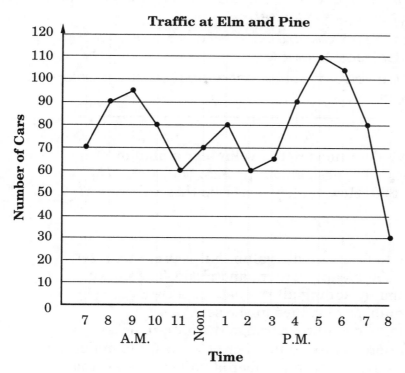

Traffic at Elm and Pine

7. At what time was the traffic heaviest? _____

8. The town can afford to place a traffic officer at this location
for one two-hour period each day. What would be the best
time for the traffic officer to be there? _____

Write About It

9. Write a paragraph telling how graphs can help you
understand data.

_____

_____

_____

9•4 Finding the Mean, Median, and Mode

Annette recorded one day's donations to the volunteer ambulance service. She received checks for these amounts: $25, $50, $25, $25, $40, $100, $15, $25, $50, $60. How can she describe this set of data?

New Idea

There are three ways to find a single value that represents a set of data. The values are called mean, median, and mode. The **mean** (meen), or average, is found by adding all the data in a set and dividing the sum by the number of values in the set.

To find the **median** (MEE-dee-uhn), arrange the data in order from least to greatest. If there is an odd number of values, the middle value is the median. If there is an even number of values, the average of the two middle values is the median.

The **mode** (mohd) is the value or values that appear most often in the set. A set in which all the values are different has no mode.

Examples: Find the mean, median, and mode amounts of the checks Annette received.

$$\text{mean} = \frac{\text{sum of values}}{\text{number of values}}$$

$$= \frac{25 + 50 + 25 + 25 + 40 + 100 + 15 + 25 + 50 + 60}{10}$$

$$= \frac{415}{10}$$

$$= 41.5$$

The mean check amount is $41.50.

To find the median, arrange the data in order:
15, 25, 25, 25, 25, 40, 50, 50, 60, 100.

There is an even number of values. The two middle values are 25 and 40.

$$\frac{(25 + 40)}{2} = 32.5 \qquad \leftarrow \quad \text{Add and divide by 2.}$$

The median check amount is $32.50.

Use the list of data arranged in order to find the mode. The value that appears most often is 25.

The mode of the check amounts is $25.00.

◄ Focus on the Idea

The mean of a set of data is found by adding the values and dividing by the number of values. The median is the middle value of a set of data arranged in order. The mode is the value or values that occur most often.

Practice

Find the mean, median, and mode of each set of data. The first one is done for you.

1. 29, 36, 45, 28, 36, 54
   Mean: _____38_____
   Median: _____36_____
   Mode: _____36_____

2. 9, 8, 8, 9, 7, 6
   Mean: _____
   Median: _____
   Mode: _____

3. 2, 4, 4, 3, 5, 1, 4, 3, 2, 4
   Mean: _____
   Median: _____
   Mode: _____

4. 70, 89, 86, 100, 92, 98, 81
   Mean: _____
   Median: _____
   Mode: _____

Apply the Idea

5. Rick is a consumer reporter for a newspaper. He found these per-pound prices for ground beef at five different supermarkets: $2.39, $2.45, $2.25, $1.99, $2.25. Find the mean, median, and mode of the prices.

   _____

✎ Write About It

6. In a set of data like 2, 4, 2, 4, 25, which measure (mean, median, or mode) do you think gives the most useful representation for all the data? Explain your answer.

   _____

◀9•5 Finding Probability

◀ IN THIS LESSON, YOU WILL LEARN

To find the probability of an event

To find an experimental probability

WORDS TO LEARN

Experiment *an activity in which the results can be recorded*

Possible outcomes *all the results that could occur in an experiment*

Event *one particular outcome of all possible outcomes*

Favorable outcome *a result that matches the chosen event*

Probability of an event *the ratio of the number of favorable outcomes to the total number of possible outcomes*

Experimental probability *the probability of an event based on actual data*

While on his way to the fruit stand, Francisco was tossing a quarter in the air and catching it. René saw him and said that the probability of getting heads is one-half. Francisco did not believe René, so they decided to toss the coin ten times and record the number of heads. Out of the 10 tosses, 7 were heads. Since 7 out of 10 is more than half, Francisco said that René was wrong. Who is right?

New Idea

An activity in which the results can be recorded is called an **experiment** (ehks-PAIR-uh-mehnt). The **possible outcomes** (PAHS-uh-buhl OWT-kuhmz) of an experiment are all the results that could occur. One particular outcome of the possible outcomes is called an **event.** (ee-VEHNT). When a result matches the chosen event, it is a **favorable outcome** (FAY-vor-uh-buhl). The **probability of an event** (prohb-uh-BIHL-uh-tee) is the ratio of the number of favorable outcomes to the total number of possible outcomes. When an event is impossible, its probability is 0. When an event is certain to happen, its probability is 1. The expression $P(E)$ stands for the probability of an event.

Examples: With one toss, what is the probability that a coin lands on heads?

12

124

56

811

111

There are 2 possible outcomes for tossing a coin, heads or tails. There is 1 favorable outcome, heads. The probability of heads, or $P(\text{H}) = \frac{1}{2}$, or 0.5.

↪Remember

To express a fraction as a decimal, divide the numerator by the denominator: $1 \div 2 = 0.5$

Example: Frank's Deli is offering its first 50 customers a choice of 50 balloons. Three of the balloons contain a card that says "Free Lunch Today." What is the probability that the first customer will get a free lunch?

$$P(\text{free lunch}) = \frac{\text{Balloons with cards}}{\text{Total balloons}}$$

$$= \frac{3}{50}$$

$$= 0.06$$

The probability of the first customer's getting a free lunch is 3 out of 50, 0.06, or 6%.

What is the probability that the first customer will not get a free lunch?

$$P(\text{no free lunch}) = \frac{\text{Balloons without cards}}{\text{Total balloons}}$$

$$= \frac{47}{50}$$

$$= 0.94$$

The probability of the first customer's not getting a free lunch is 47 out of 50, 0.94, or 94%.

✓Check the Math

1. The first customer won a free lunch! Al is the second customer. He thinks that the probability of his getting a free lunch is $\frac{2}{49}$. Is Al correct? Why or why not?

_____

_____

◢Focus on the Idea

The probability of an event is the ratio of the number of favorable outcomes to the number of all possible outcomes. Probability is always a number between 0 and 1.

Practice

Find the probability of each outcome for the experiment described. The first one is done for you.

Experiment 1: In an envelope, there are 10 cards: 3 red, 5 blue, and 2 yellow. Without looking, choose a card from the envelope; then put it back in the envelope. What is the probability of choosing each color?

2. $P(\text{red}) = \underline{\ \frac{3}{10}\text{ or }0.3\ }$ **3.** $P(\text{yellow}) = \underline{\hspace{2cm}}$

4. $P(\text{blue}) = \underline{\hspace{2cm}}$ **5.** $P(\text{orange}) = \underline{\hspace{2cm}}$

Experiment 2: Imagine spinning this spinner once. Write the probability of each event in exercises 6 to 9.

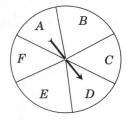

6. $P(C) = \underline{\hspace{2cm}}$ **7.** $P(A \text{ or } E) = \underline{\hspace{2cm}}$

8. $P(\text{consonant}) = \underline{\hspace{2cm}}$ **9.** $P(\text{letter before } G \text{ in alphabet}) = \underline{\hspace{2cm}}$

Experiment 3: A number cube (or die—one of a pair of dice) with 6 sides numbered from 1 to 6 is rolled. Write the probability of each event.

10. $P(4) = \underline{\hspace{2cm}}$ **11.** $P(\text{number greater than 4}) = \underline{\hspace{2cm}}$

12. $P(\text{odd number}) = \underline{\hspace{2cm}}$ **13.** $P(12) = \underline{\hspace{2cm}}$

Extend the Idea

Francisco thinks that because he tossed the coin 10 times and got heads 7 times, $P(\text{heads}) = \frac{7}{10}$, or 0.7. Francisco is finding the **experimental probability** (ehks-pair-uh-MEHNT-uhl prahb-uh-BIHL-uh-tee), which is the probability based on actual data that he has observed.

Example: René said that Francisco should toss the coin 10 more times. Francisco tossed 4 heads and 6 tails. Now what is the experimental probability of getting heads?

He tossed 7 heads and now 4 heads, so there are 11 favorable outcomes. Because Francisco has tossed the coin a total of 20 times, he now has an experimental probability of $\frac{11}{20}$, or 0.55.

✓Check Your Understanding

14. Francisco tossed the coin 10 more times. He got 5 heads and 5 tails. Now what is his experimental probability of getting heads? $\underline{\hspace{2cm}}$

Practice

15. Four different coins are in a hat. One coin is picked without looking, then replaced. After picking 50 times, the penny was picked 4 times, the nickel 23 times, the dime 17 times, and the quarter 6 times. Find the experimental probability of each event. The first one is done for you.

    a. $P(\text{nickel}) = \frac{23}{50}$ or 0.46   **b.** $P(\text{dime}) = $ _____

    c. $P(\text{quarter}) = $ _____   **d.** $P(\text{penny}) = $ _____

16. One hundred people were asked to name their favorite fruit. The results are in the table.

Fruit	Number of People	Fruit	Number of People
Peach	25	Orange	20
Pear	11	Other fruit	44

    Based on this data, find the experimental probability that the next person's favorite fruit is:

    a. a peach _____   **b.** a pear _____

    c. an orange _____   **d.** other fruit _____

Apply the Idea

17. Mike's Music Store is giving one customer each day a choice of a free cassette or CD. So far, 5 winners have chosen cassettes and 15 have chosen CDs. What is the experimental probability that the next winner will choose a CD?

    _____

18. Toss a coin 50 times. Record the number of heads and the number of tails. What is the experimental probability that your next toss will be heads? _____

Write About It

19. Francisco and René continued their discussion. After 100 tosses, Francisco had counted 54 heads and 46 tails. After 1,000 tosses, Francisco had counted 475 heads and 525 tails, so that $P(\text{heads}) = \frac{475}{1,000} = \frac{19}{40}$, or 0.475. René still says that $P(\text{heads}) = \frac{1}{2}$, or 0.5. Who do you think is correct? Explain.

    _____

    _____

20. Why must the probability of an event always be between 0 and 1?

    _____

    _____

Chapter 9 Review

In This Chapter, You Have Learned

- To organize data into frequency tables and histograms
- To read tables and use them to solve problems
- To read and interpret bar, line, and circle graphs
- To find the mean, median, and mode of a set of data
- To find the probability of an event
- To find an experimental probability

Words You Know

From the lists of "Words to Learn," choose the word or phrase that best completes each statement.

1. A(n) _____ table can record the number of times a score is repeated.

2. The _____ of a set of scores is found by adding all the scores and dividing by the number of scores.

3. The _____ is the score or scores that are repeated most often.

4. A(n) _____ records changes in data with plotted points connected by straight lines.

5. The probability of an event is the ratio of the number of favorable outcomes to the number of _____ .

More Practice

Complete the frequency table for each group of data.

6. T-shirt sizes sold:
    M, S, S, M, M, M, L, S,
    M, L, L, M, L, M, L, L

    S: _____

    M: _____

    L: _____

7. Heights of plants after two weeks:
    1.2 cm, 2.1 cm, 1.7 cm, 1.5 cm, 0.9 cm,
    2.5 cm, 3.1 cm, 2.7 cm, 2.2 cm, 3.4 cm

    0 – 1 cm: _____

    1 – 2 cm: _____

    2 – 3 cm: _____

    3 – 4 cm: _____

8. Make a histogram for the data in exercise 6.

Use the graphs to answer these questions.

9. What was Judy's sales total for the week? _____

10. What was the total sales made by all four representatives? _____

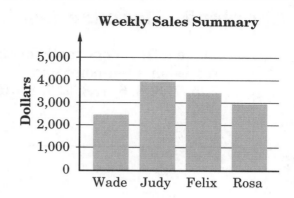

Weekly Sales Summary

11. Estimate the highest temperature of the day.
_____

12. During which 2-hour period did the temperature increase the most? _____

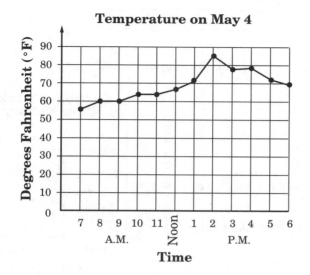

Temperature on May 4

13. What percent of all computers are in use in the United States and Japan? _____

14. If the total number of computers in use is 148 million, about how many computers are in use in Europe? (Hint: Start by rounding the given percentage to the nearest whole number.)

_____

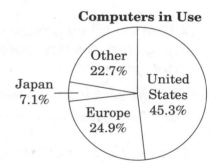

Computers in Use

Other 22.7%
Japan 7.1%
Europe 24.9%
United States 45.3%

Find the mean, median, and mode for each set of data.

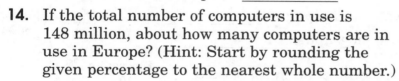

15. 98, 90, 82, 100, 83

Mean: _____

Median: _____

Mode: _____

16. 3, 2, 2, 2, 5, 15, 1, 2

Mean: _____

Median: _____

Mode: _____

Problems You Can Solve

17. Of the 12,000 light bulbs produced in a factory, 450 were found to be imperfect. What is the experimental probability that the next light bulb will be imperfect? _____

18. A die is rolled. What is the probability that the number rolled is less than 5? _____

19. **For Your Portfolio** Find a graph in a newspaper or magazine. Identify the graph. Make up three questions about it. Exchange questions and graphs with a partner and answer each other's questions.

Chapter 9   Practice Test

1. Make a frequency table for the scores on a ten-point quiz:
5, 5, 7, 8, 8, 6, 7, 8, 7, 7, 8, 10, 9

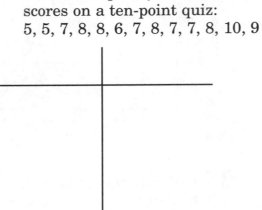

2. Make a histogram for the scores in exercise 1.

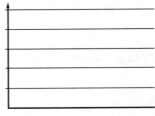

3. How many workers at Miller Factory walk to work? _____

4. How many workers in all are represented on this graph? _____

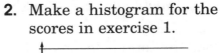

A librarian asked patrons which kind of books they like to read. The responses of 600 people are reflected in the circle graph.

5. Which kind of book was most popular? _____

6. How many people chose biographies? _____

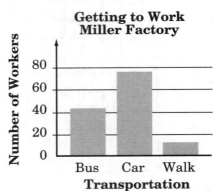

Find the mean, median, and mode for each set of data.

7. 25, 50, 45, 38, 25
Mean: _____
Median: _____
Mode: _____

8. 300, 150, 200, 200, 500, 650, 100
Mean: _____
Median: _____
Mode: _____

An envelope contains 5 red cards, 7 blue cards, and 11 yellow cards. A card is chosen without looking, then replaced. What is the probability of choosing each color card?

9. P(Red) = _____   10. P(Yellow) = _____   11. P(Green) = _____

A baseball player had these results from his last 100 times at bat:

Singles: 22   Doubles: 5   Home runs: 2   Outs: 71

Find the experimental probability that in his next time at bat, this player will:

12. get a single _____

13. make an out _____

14. get a home run _____

15. not make an out _____

Glossary

A

Area measure of a flat region inside a figure (5•3)

Acre a special unit of area used in land measurements (5•3)

Actuary a person who uses mathematics and statistics to make predictions for insurance companies (7•5)

Addition Property of 0 states that 0 added to any number does not change the number (1•4)

Addition Property of Equality a rule stating that the same number can be added to each side of an equation (2•2)

Associative Property of Addition states that the grouping of numbers being added does not affect the sum (1•4)

Associative Property of Multiplication states that the grouping of numbers being multiplied does not affect the product (1•4)

B

Bar graph a graph that records and compares data, using bars (9•3)

Base a number multiplied by itself (4•1)

Binomial a polynomial with two terms (4•4)

Board foot a unit for measuring lumber that is equal to 12 inches by 12 inches by 1 inch (6•5)

C

Check a solution substituting a number or numbers for the variable or variables in the original equation (2•3)

Circle graph a graph that shows the relationship of parts of data to the whole (9•3)

Coefficient the number part of a monomial (4•3)

Common denominator a common multiple of two or more denominators (5•1)

Common factors numbers or variables that are factors of two or more monomials (4•3)

Commutative Property of Addition states that the order of numbers being added does not affect the sum (1•4)

Commutative Property of Multiplication states that the order of numbers being multiplied does not affect the product (1•4)

Composite number a whole number that has more than two factors (4•2)

Constant a monomial with no variables (4•3)

Coordinate a number that locates a position along a number line (8•2)

Coordinate plane a flat region formed by two perpendicular number lines (8•2)

Cross-products in the proportion $\frac{a}{b} = \frac{c}{d}$ the cross-products are ad and bc (7•2)

D

Decimal a number that represents a fraction with a denominator that is a power of ten (6•1)

Deduct to take away or subtract from (3•5)

Denominator the number below the fraction bar in a fraction (4•6)

Deposit to put in or add to (3•5)

Discount an amount by which the regular cost is reduced (9•2)

Distributive Property of Multiplication Over Addition states that there are two ways to find the product of a number and a sum (1•5)

Division Property of Equality a rule stating that if each side of an equation is divided by the same nonzero number, the sides are still equal (2•5)

Dowels small, round rods used to stabilize a larger structure (6•3)

E

Elevation the height of an object or place (3•4)

Equation a statement that two expressions are equal (2•1)

Equation with two variables an equation that expresses the relationship between two quantities (8•3)

Equivalent decimals two decimals with the same value (6•1)

Equivalent fractions fractions that have the same value (4•6)

Equivalent ratios ratios that have the same value (7•1)

Evaluate to find the value of a variable expression (1•3)

Event one particular outcome from all possible outcomes (9•5)

Experiment an activity in which the results can be recorded (9•5)

Experimental probability the probability of an event based on actual data (9•5)

Exponent indicates the number of times a base is multiplied by itself to produce a product (4•1)

F

Factor a number that is multiplied by another number to produce a product (4•1)

Favorable outcome a result that matches the chosen event (9•5)

Fraction a number that describes a part of a whole (4•6)

Frequency table a table that shows how often a certain data value occurs (9•1)

G

Graph of an equation the set of all points that are solutions to an equation (8•4)

Graph of a solution use a number line to show the solution to an equation (8•1)

Greatest common factor (GCF) the largest number that evenly divides two or more other numbers (4•5)

H

Histogram a graph of the data in a frequency table (9•1)

I

Identity Property for Multiplication a rule that states that any number multiplied by 1 equals itself (5•3)

Improper fraction a fraction in which the numerator is equal to or greater than the denominator (5•1)

Inequality symbols the symbols that are used to compare two numbers (3•2)

Inverse operations mathematical operations that reverse, or "undo" each other (2•2)

L

Least common multiple (LCM) the smallest number that is a multiple of two or more given numbers (4•7)

Like terms terms that have the same variable and the same exponent (4•4)

Line graph a graph that records changes in data with plotted points connected by straight lines (9•3)

Lowest terms a fraction is in lowest terms if it has no common factor other than 1 in its numerator and denominator (4•6)

M

Mathematical expression a combination of numbers and symbols (1•1)

Mean the sum of a set of data divided by the number of values in the set (9•4)

Median the middle value of a set of data arranged in order from least to greatest (9•4)

Meteorology the science of observing and predicting weather (7•6)

Micrometer a device to measure very small objects (6•1)

Mixed number a combination of a whole number and a fraction (5•1)

Mode the value or values that appear most often in a set of data (9•4)

Monomial a number, a variable, or a product of numbers and variables (4•3)

Multiple a number that is the product of a given number and any whole number (4•7)

Multiplication Property of 0 states that any number multiplied by 0 has a product of 0 (1•4)

Multiplication Property of 1 states that multiplying any number by 1 does not change the number (1•4)

Multiplication Property of Equality a rule stating that if each side of an equation is multiplied by the same number, the sides are still equal (2•4)

N

Negative number a number that is less than 0 (3•1)

Number line diagram on which positive and negative numbers and zero can be located (3•2)

Numerator the number above the fraction bar in a fraction (4•6)

O

One-step equation an equation that can be solved in a single operation (3•7)

Opposite numbers two numbers that are the same distance from zero on a number line, but in opposite directions (3•2)

Order of operations rules for performing mathematical operations in expressions having more than one operation (1•1)

Ordered pair two numbers that name the x-coordinate and the y-coordinate of a point (8•2)

Origin the point at which the x-axis and the y-axis meet (8•2)

P

Percent a ratio that compares a number to 100 (7•4)

Polynomial a monomial or the sum or difference of two or more monomials (4•4)

Positive number a number that is greater than 0 (3•1)

Possible outcomes all the results that could occur in an experiment (9•5)

Prime factorization the value of a composite number written as a product of its prime numbers (4•2)

Prime number a whole number whose only factors are 1 and the number itself (4•2)

Probability of an event the ratio of the number of favorable outcomes to the total number of possible outcomes (9•5)

Proportion a statement that two ratios are equal (7•2)

R

Rate a special kind of ratio that compares quantities of two different units (7•1)

Ratio a comparison of two quantities (7•1)

Reciprocals two numbers are reciprocals if their product is 1 (5•4)

Related sentences number sentences that involve inverse operations (3•6)

Rename to write a number in a different form (5•2)

S

Solution the value of the variable that makes an equation true (2•1)

T

Term another name for a monomial (4•4)

Trinomial a polynomial with three terms (4•4)

U

Unit a single quantity of measurement (3•3)

V

Variable a letter used to represent one or more unknown numbers (1•2)

Variable expression an expression that includes numbers, variables, and mathematical symbols (1•2)

Vertical form the alignment of two or more decimals so that their decimal points and place values are lined up vertically (6•2)

X

x-axis the horizontal number line on a coordinate plane (8•2)

Y

y-axis the vertical number line on a coordinate plane

Answers

Chapter 1 Introduction to Algebra

1•1 Using Order of Operations

1. Divide 21 by 3. 3. Multiplication 5. Division
7. Division 9. Addition 11. 31 13. 45 15. 135
17. 36 19. 58 21. 26
23. a. $9 + 3(2)$; $9 + 6$; 15
    b. $40 - [6 + 2(15)]$; $40 - [6 + 30]$; $40 - 36$; 4
25. $20 - 11$; 9 27. $10 + 3(4)$; $10 + 12$; 22
29. $40 - 4(7)$; $40 - 28$; 12 31. $4(8) \div 4$; $32 \div 4$; 8
33. 9 35. 88 37. 10 39. 22 41. 6
43. a. $275 b. First multiply from left to right. Then add from left to right.

1•2 Writing Expressions

1. b 3. c 5. t; $4t$

1•3 Evaluating Expressions

1. 14 3. 177 5. 11 7. 11; 15; 18; 22
9. 5; 10; 12; 20 11. a. $c + $2 b. $16

1•4 Using Properties of Operations

1. Commutative. First exchange the $110 and the $325. Then add from left to right.
3. Associative Property of Addition
5. Associative Property of Addition
7. 335 9. 39
11. Associative and commutative. First change $13 \cdot 2$ to $2 \cdot 13$. Then move the parentheses from $5(2 \cdot 13)$ to $(5 \cdot 2) \cdot 13$.
13. Commutative Property of Multiplication
15. Associative Property of Multiplication
17. 2,400 19. 70

1•5 Using the Distributive Property of Multiplication Over Addition

1. b 3. Yes 5. $9(4 + 6) = 90$
7. $(16 \cdot 10) + (16 \cdot 3) = 208$
9. $(256 \cdot 100) + (256 \cdot 2) = 26{,}112$

Chapter 1 Review

1. b 2. c 3. d 4. h 5. e 6. f 7. g 8. a 9. 24
10. 30 11. 18 12. 48 13. 40 14. 73 15. b
16. c 17. 20 18. 27 19. 5 20. 17
21. Commutative Property of Addition
22. Distributive Property of Multiplication Over Addition
23. Multiplication Property of 1
24. Associative Property of Multiplication
25. Multiplication Property of 0
26. Commutative Property of Multiplication
27. Possible answer: Use the Commutative Property of Multiplication to change $11 \cdot 6$ to $6 \cdot 11$, then use the Associative Property of Multiplication to get $5(6 \cdot 11) = (5 \cdot 6)11 = 330$.
28. Use the Distributive Property of Multiplication Over Addition to get $8(32 + 18) = 8(50) = 400$.
29. a. $60h b. $420 30. $72

Chapter 2 Equations

2•1 Using Equations

1. No 3. Yes 5. No 7. b 9. b 11. a 13. c
15. $0.20p = 34.60$; 173 pieces

2•2 Solving Equations By Adding

1. Add 5 counters to the second group.
3. $b + 20 = 35$ 5. $s + 17 = 33$ 7. $y + 1 = 8$
9. $c + 23 = 62$ 11. Subtract 41. 13. Add 19.
15. Add 8. 17. $z = 23$ 19. $h = 531$ 21. 13; 89
23. 11; 21 25. $x = 158$ 27. $x = 38$ 29. $x = 178$
31. $x = 104$ 33. $x - 80 = 4{,}02.9$; $4,109

2•3 Solving Equations By Subtracting

1. $b = 8$ **3.** $c = 15$ **5.** $e = 26$ **7.** $k = 35$ **9.** $o = 60$
11. a. $h = 72$ **b.** She has to volunteer another 72 hours to fulfill her obligation.

2•4 Solving Equations By Multiplying

1. $r = 150$ **3.** $y = 21$ **5.** $w = 48$ **7.** $a = 90$
9. $b = 184$ **11.** $h = 500$ **13.** $\frac{x}{6} = 21$; $126

2•5 Solving Equations By Dividing

1. Divide both sides of the equation by 9.
3. $x = 12$ **5.** $x = 6$ **7.** $b = 11$ **9.** $d = 73$
11. $h = 34$ **13.** $l = 17$
15. 21 has been subtracted from x to get 70.
17. x has been divided by 2 to get 18.
19. x has been multiplied by 4 to get 72.
21. $g = 37$ **23.** $i = 9$ **25.** $l = 25$ **27.** $n = 111$
29. $d = 151$ **31.** $f = 77$ **33.** a **35.** b
37. $6x = 174$; 29 extension cards

Chapter 2 Review

1. equation **2.** solution **3.** inverse operations
4. Multiplication Property of Equality
5. b **6.** c **7.** b **8.** c **9.** 3 **10.** 8 **11.** 100
12. 103 **13.** 3 **14.** 13 **15.** 72 **16.** 8 **17.** 21
18. 9 **19.** -48 **20.** 216 **21.** $350
22. $2,100 **23.** $2,000

Chapter 3 Positive and Negative Numbers

3•1 Using Positive and Negative Numbers

1. -25 lb **3.** $+40$ yd **5.** -25 yd **7.** $+12{,}000$ ft
9. -12 steps **11.** -25 m **13.** $+15$ steps
15. $+15$ ft **17.** -14 gal
19. a. $+2$ stamps **b.** -4 stamps **c.** -1 stamp
     d. $+12$ stamps **e.** -7 stamps

3•2 Using a Number Line

1. $>$ **3.** $<$ **5.** $<$ **7.** -8 **9.** -1 **11.** -3 **13.** 4
15. 11 **17.** Tokyo

3•3 Adding Positive and Negative Numbers

1. No. $-11 + 20 = 9$ **3.** $-4 + (-5) = -9$
5. $8 + (-5) = 3$
7. -4

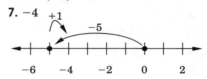

9. 3

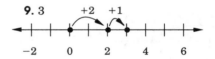

11. 1

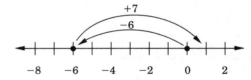

13. -8

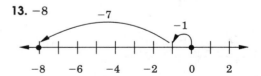

15. $-2 + 5 = 3$ **17.** $-2 + (-1) = -3$ **19.** -8
21. 3 **23.** -3 **25.** -7 **27.** -9 **29.** 5 **31.** 15 ft

3•4 Subtracting Positive and Negative Numbers

1. Possible answer: Go from 0 to the number, and then back again to 0. One will always get 0 as the answer.

3. $2 - 5 = -3$

5. -9

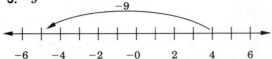

7. -2

9. 2

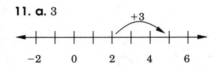

11. a. 3

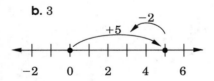

b. 3

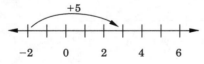

13. a. 5

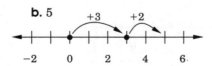

b. 5

15. Yes. Possible answer: $-5 - (-25) = 20$

17. 5; -2 19. 1; -3 21. -11 23. 8 25. -8

3•5 Multiplying Positive and Negative Numbers

1. -10 3. -27 5. -21 7. -16 9. -45
11. 270 13. $-12°$

3•6 Dividing Positive and Negative Numbers

1. -3; -3 3. 8; 8 5. -6 7. 15 9. -50
11. -141 13. -200 15. 12

3•7 Solving Equations Using Positive and Negative Numbers

1. $x = -17$ 3. $x = 20$ 5. $x = -6$ 7. $x = -10$
9. $x = -7$ 11. $x = -24$ 13. b; $x = 4°$ per hour

Chapter 3 Review

1. inequality symbols 2. negative
3. positive 4. $-3,000$ ft 5. $+6°$ 6. $+50$ yd
7. $+97$ 8. -4 9. 2 10. -1 11. -2 12. -5
13. 15 14. > 15. > 16. < 17. -11 18. -3 19. 6
20. 7 21. -4 22. -11 23. -5 24. 14 25. -25
26. -28 27. 44 28. -300 29. -7 30. 9 31. -5
32. -4 33. $x = -16$ 34. $x = -26$ 35. $x = -6$
36. $x = -30$ 37. -6 °F
38. 13 ft higher than the starting point

Chapter 4   Factors and Fractions

4•1   Evaluating Expressions with Exponents

1.

Statement	Base	Exponent	Product
$3^4 = 81$	3	4	81
$5^2 = 25$	5	2	25
$7^3 = 343$	7	3	343

3. 27   **5.** 16   **7.** -1 **9.** -64 **11.** 44   **13.** -14
15. 54   **17.** -21 **19.** -9 **21.** -3
23. -2; 0; -8; -18 **25.** 9; 10; 9; 6
27. 0; -1; 0; 15   **29. a.** B   **b.** 72

4•2   Finding Prime Factors

1. P   **3.** C   **5.** C   **7.** P   **9.** 2 • 13
11. 2^2 • 11   **13.** 2^2 • 7
15. Possible answer:

$2^2 \cdot 3^2$

17.

2^3

19. Three equal layers of 16 rows with 1 can in each
row, three equal layers of 8 rows with 2 cans in
each row, three equal layers of 4 rows with 4 cans
in each row, three equal layers of 2 rows with 8
cans in each row, or three equal layers of 1 row
with 16 cans in each row.

4•3   Identifying Monomials and Their Factors

1. Yes   **3.** No   **5.** Yes   **7.** 1   **9.** 2   **11.** -1
13. -1 **15.** c   **17.** b

4•4   Identifying and Simplifying Polynomials

1. c   **3.** b   **5.** Not possible   **7.** $8x^2$
9. $19y^2 - 3y$ **11.** $3y + 5x$

4•5   Finding the Greatest Common Factor

1. 2   **3.** 2   **5.** 3   **7.** 3   **9.** 3   **11.** 4   **13.** 9
15. Possible answer: 6 and 12   **17.** 1 and 2

4•6   Writing Fractions in Lowest Terms

1. 54
3.

5.

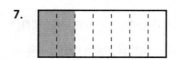

7.

9. No   **11.** Yes   **13.** Yes   **15.** $\frac{4}{5}$ **17.** $\frac{5}{6}$ **19.** $\frac{7}{8}$
21. $\frac{2}{3}$ **23.** $\frac{1}{3}$ **25.** $\frac{7}{8}$ **27. a.** 12   **b.** $\frac{1}{3}$; $\frac{2}{3}$; $\frac{3}{3}$

4•7   Finding the Least Common Multiple

1. 4   **3.** 8   **5.** 60   **7.** $\frac{2}{6}$; $\frac{3}{6}$ **9.** $\frac{2}{8}$; $\frac{3}{8}$ **11.** $\frac{6}{16}$

Chapter 4 Review

1. monomial   **2.** binomial   **3.** common factor
4. coefficient   **5.** trinomial   **6.** exponent   **7.** 9
8. -27 **9.** 25   **10.** 53   **11.** -24 **12.** 2^2 • 7   **13.** 2^5
14. 2 • 3 • 7   **15.** 3^2 • 5   **16.** 3   **17.** -4 **18.** $\frac{4}{5}$
19. $8a - 3$ **20.** $13x^2 - 2x$ **21.** 2   **22.** 5   **23.** 6   **24.** $\frac{8}{15}$
25. $\frac{4}{9}$ **26.** 14   **27.** 30   **28.** $\frac{5}{10}$; $\frac{6}{10}$ **29.** $\frac{9}{12}$; $\frac{1}{12}$
30. 60 ft • 1 ft, 20 ft • 3 ft, 15 ft • 4 ft, 12 ft • 5 ft,
10 ft • 6 ft
31. $\frac{5}{24}$

Chapter 5   Solving Equations with Fractions

5•1   Solving Equations by Adding Fractions

1. $\frac{10}{15}$, $\frac{3}{15}$, $\frac{13}{15}$ **3.** $\frac{5}{9}$ **5.** $\frac{3}{4}$ **7.** $\frac{2}{3}$ **9.** $\frac{7}{15}$ **11.** $\frac{7}{20}$
13. $\frac{7}{12}$ **15.** $\frac{7}{8}$ **17.** $3\frac{1}{2}$ **19.** $13\frac{1}{4}$ **21.** $7\frac{1}{2}$ **23.** 37
25. $4\frac{3}{4}$ **27.** 2   **29.** $4\frac{1}{12}$ **31.** $\frac{7}{8}$ in.   **33.** $42\frac{3}{4}$ in.

5•2   Solving Equations by Subtracting Fractions

1. $\frac{1}{6}$ **3.** $\frac{3}{8}$ **5.** $\frac{2}{3}$ **7.** $\frac{3}{10}$ **9.** $\frac{5}{12}$ **11.** $\frac{1}{2}$
13. $1\frac{1}{7}$ **15.** $\frac{3}{10}$ **17.** $2\frac{3}{4}$ ft

5•3   Solving Equations by Multiplying

1. No. Possible answer: To multiply, you only need to multiply the numerators and the denominators. Common denominators are needed only for addition and subtraction.
3. $\frac{7}{10}$ **5.** $\frac{10}{21}$ **7.** $\frac{1}{12}$ **9.** $\frac{1}{16}$
11. No. Possible answer: Jill may have used the shortcut on the 2 and the 8, but you cannot use the shortcut when both numbers are in the denominator.
13. $10\frac{1}{2}$ **15.** $3\frac{3}{10}$ **17.** $2\frac{5}{8}$ **19.** $10\frac{2}{3}$ **21.** 10
23. $16\frac{1}{2}$ yd^2 **25.** about 750

5•4   Solving Equations by Dividing Fractions

1. $\frac{3}{2}$ **3.** $-\frac{5}{4}$ **5.** $\frac{8}{1}$ **7.** $-\frac{5}{6}$ **9.** $-\frac{5}{16}$ **11.** 2   **13.** 18
15. $4\frac{2}{3}$ **17.** 90

Chapter 5 Review

1. common denominator
2. Identity Property for Multiplication
3. improper fraction   **4.** mixed number
5. reciprocals   **6.** $\frac{5}{7}$ **7.** $\frac{7}{10}$ **8.** $\frac{5}{8}$ **9.** $\frac{1}{8}$ **10.** $5\frac{7}{12}$
11. $3\frac{5}{8}$ **12.** $7\frac{5}{8}$ **13.** $2\frac{1}{2}$ **14.** $\frac{2}{15}$ **15.** 8   **16.** $\frac{5}{12}$ **17.** $1\frac{1}{2}$
18. $\frac{2}{9}$ **19.** $2\frac{1}{2}$ **20.** $3\frac{1}{2}$ **21.** $\frac{4}{5}$ **22.** $9\frac{5}{8}$ **23.** $\frac{5}{8}$ **24.** $\frac{1}{2}$
25. 14   **26.** $1\frac{3}{10}$ **27.** $3\frac{1}{3}$ **28.** $4\frac{1}{6}$ ft   **29. a.** 10   **b.** 4

Chapter 6   Solving Equations with Decimals

6•1   Finding Equivalent Decimals and Fractions

1. Less than. Possible answer: A number with only one tenth is less than a number with two tenths.
3. 0.12   **5.** <   **7.** >   **9.** >**11.** Yes   **13.** No
15. $\frac{9}{100}$ **17.** $\frac{3}{4}$ **19.** $\frac{3}{25}$ **21.** 0.8   **23.** 0.06
25. 0.24   **27.** 0.027

6•2   Adding Decimals

1. 0.7   **3.** 27.272   **5.** 10.95   **7.** 66.043
9. 4.3   **11.** 8.62

6•3   Subtracting Decimals

1. 0.3   **3.** 1.87   **5.** 16.76   **7.** 2.2
9. 2.5   **11.** $6.50

6•4   Multiplying Decimals

1. 3.6   **3.** 0.0024   **5.** 0.975   **7.** 9   **9.** 4.2
11. a. 61.88 yd^2 **b.** $1,500.59

6•5   Dividing Decimals

1. 3 planks   **3.** 0.41   **5.** 0.078   **7.** 1.568
9. 0.3   **11.** 31.70   **13.** 0.05   **15.** 23.2
17. 1,405   **19.** 3.2   **21.** 1.55   **23.** 2.4
25. 0.6   **27.** 1.7 kg   **29.** 9

Chapter 6 Review

1. equivalent   **2.** vertical form   **3.** factor   **4.** decimal
5. 0.7   **6.** 0.24   **7.** >   **8.** <   **9.** >   **10.** 0.25
11. $0.8\overline{3}$ **12.** 0.8   **13.** 23.2   **14.** 14.6   **15.** 6.6   **16.** 0.8
17. 68.48   **18.** 4.3   **19.** 0.18   **20.** 5.74   **21.** 0.021
22. 0.3   **23.** 30   **24.** 60.4   **25.** 0.74   **26.** 13.8   **27.** 9.47
28. 5.203   **29.** 4.65   **30.** 6.2   **31.** 7.8 pounds
32. $18.38   **33.** 0.804 meter   **34.** 499.6 gallons
35. 48 words per minute

Chapter 7   Proportions and Percents

7•1   Understanding Ratio

1. $\frac{4}{1}$ **3.** $\frac{2}{1}$ **5.** 30 mi/h   **7.** \$6.40/pound
9. 20 mi/gal   **11.** $\frac{4}{5}$ **13.** $\frac{9}{25}$

7•2   Using Ratio and Proportion

1. No   **3.** Yes   **5.** Yes   **7.** No
9. Yes   **11.** Yes   **13.** $\frac{12}{6} = \frac{4}{2}$

7•3   Solving Proportions

1. 6   **3.** 5   **5.** 6
7. b; 125 quarts of whole milk
9. b; 180 minutes or 3 hours

7•4   Understanding Percent

1. 3%   **3.** 71%   **5.** 21%   **7.** 102%   **9.** 100%
11. 175%   **13.** $\frac{3}{20}$; 0.15   **15.** $\frac{7}{100}$; 0.07
17. 4%   **19.** 25%

7•5   Using Proportions with Percents

1. $\frac{225}{300} = \frac{x}{100}$ **3.** $\frac{97.5}{150} = \frac{x}{100}$ **5.** Yes
7. $\frac{30}{100} = \frac{x}{90}$ **9.** $\frac{45}{100} = \frac{x}{200}$

7•6   Solving Percent Problems

1. $\frac{25}{300} = \frac{x}{100}$; 8.3%   **3.** $\frac{30}{100} = \frac{x}{90}$; 27
5. $\frac{62}{100} = \frac{x}{17,500}$; 10,850 residents
7. $\frac{3}{100} = \frac{x}{15,000}$; \$450

Chapter 7 Review

1. ratio   **2.** rate   **3.** equivalent ratios
4. proportion   **5.** cross-products   **6.** percent   **7.** $\frac{1}{2}$
8. $\frac{5}{3}$ **9.** $\frac{6}{5}$ **10.** $\frac{1}{3}$ **11.** 50 mi/h   **12.** 8 oz/serving
13. Yes   **14.** No   **15.** 21   **16.** 9   **17.** 4.4   **18.** 6   **19.** 6%
20. 50%   **21.** 60%   **22.** 180%   **23.** 80%   **24.** 2%
25. $\frac{x}{100} = \frac{3}{60}$; 5%   **26.** $\frac{15}{100} = \frac{x}{200}$; 30   **27.** $\frac{2}{100} = \frac{5}{x}$; 250
28. $\frac{6}{100} = \frac{x}{140}$; \$8.40   **29.** 8 eggs
30. 25 miles per gallon   **31.** \$1.75   **32.** 12 meters
33. 300 calories from fat

Chapter 8   Graphing Equations

8•1   Graphing Equations on a Number Line

1. −6

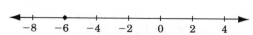

3. $\frac{-3}{4}$

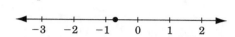

5. 0.2

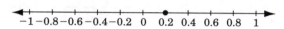

7. $q - 2 = 3$; 5 quarts

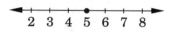

9. $\frac{l}{3} = \frac{3}{4}$; $2\frac{1}{4}$ ft

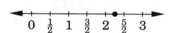

8•2   Graphing in the Coordinate Plane

1. $(-1, -2)$ **3.** $(2, 1)$ **5.** $(-2, 3)$
7., 9., 11.

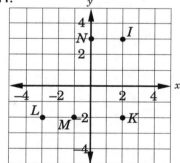

13. a. Possible answer: (1, 4), (1, 1), (1, −2), (2, −2),
(3, −2)   **b.** Answers will vary.

8•3 Solving Equations with Two Variables

1. (1, 2); (2, 3); (3, 4)

3. (1, 4); (2, 3); (3, 2)

5. (1, $3); (4, $6); (10, $12); (25, $27)

8•4 Graphing an Equation with Two Variables

1.

x	y	(x, y)
0	−1	(0, −1)
1	1	(1, 1)
2	3	(2, 3)

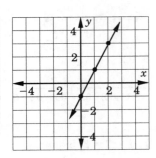

3.

x	y	(x, y)
0	3	(0, 3)
2	4	(2, 4)
4	5	(4, 5)

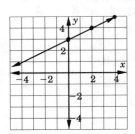

5. $40

Chapter 8 Review

1. ordered pair **2.** x-axis; y-axis **3.** origin

4. −3

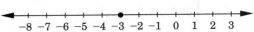

5. 2

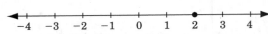

6. −1

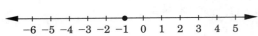

7. 3

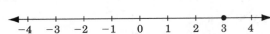

8. (0, 3) **9.** (−1, −2) **10.** (4, −1) **11.** (3, 4)

12–15.

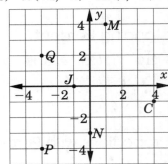

16.

x	y	(x, y)
0	3	(0, 3)
1	4	(1, 4)
2	5	(2, 5)

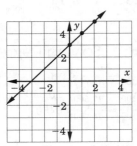

17.

x	y	(x, y)
O	-1	$(0, -1)$
1	1	$(1, 1)$
2	3	$(2, 3)$

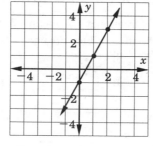

18.

x	y	(x, y)
-1	4	$(-1, 4)$
0	0	$(0, 0)$
1	-4	$(1, -4)$

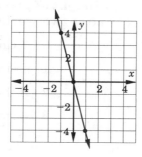

19. a.

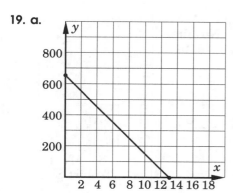

b. $500 **c.** 13 months

20. Answers will vary.

9•1 Gathering and Recording

1.

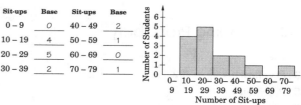

Sit-ups	Base	Sit-ups	Base
0 – 9	O	40 – 49	2
10 – 19	4	50 – 59	1
20 – 29	5	60 – 69	O
30 – 39	2	70 – 79	1

9•2 Using Graphs and Tables

1. 559,000 more dairy cows than sheep
3. 68,531,000   **5.** $12.50

9•3 Using Bar, Line, and Circle Graphs

1. January, March, November; these are winter months when the heat is used.
3. $3,000   **5.** 65%   **7.** 5 P.M.

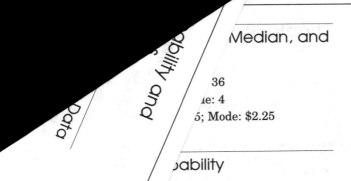

Median, and

36

...le: 4

...5; Mode: $2.25

...bability

3. 2

5. P(oran...)

7. P(A or E) $= \frac{2}{6} = \frac{1}{3} \approx 0.33$

9. P(letter before G) $= 1$

11. P(number greater than 4) $= \frac{2}{6} = \frac{1}{3} \approx 0.33$

13. $P(12) = 0$

15. a. P(nickel) $= \frac{23}{50} = 0.46$ **b.** P(dime) $= \frac{17}{50} = 0.34$
   c. P(quarter) $= \frac{6}{50} = 0.12$ **d.** P(penny) $= \frac{4}{50} = 0.08$

17. $\frac{15}{20} = \frac{3}{4} = 0.75$

Chapter 9 Review

1. frequency **2.** mean **3.** mode **4.** line graph

5. all possible outcomes

6. S: ___3___

   M: ___7___

   L: ___6___

7.

Height of plant after two weeks	Number of plants
0 – 1 cm:	1
1 – 2 cm:	3
2 – 3 cm:	4
3 – 4 cm:	2

8.

T-Shirt size	Number sold
S:	3
M:	7
L:	6

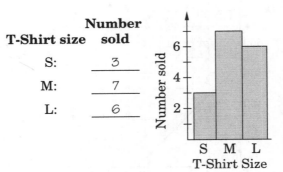

9. $4,000 **10.** $13,000 **11.** 85°F **12.** Noon–2 P.M.

13. 52.4% **14.** 36.852 million = 36,852,000

15. Mean: 90.6; Median: 90; Mode: None

16. Mean: 3.625; Median: 2; Mode: 2

17. P(imperfect) $= \frac{450}{12,000} = 0.0375$

18. P(less than 5) $= \frac{4}{6} = \frac{2}{3} \approx 0.67$

17.

x	y	(x, y)
O	-1	$(O, -1)$
1	1	$(1, 1)$
2	3	$(2, 3)$

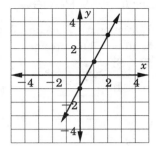

18.

x	y	(x, y)
-1	4	$(-1, 4)$
0	0	$(0, 0)$
1	-4	$(1, -4)$

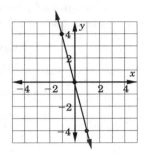

19. a.

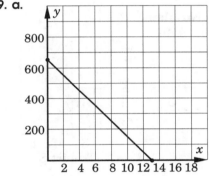

b. $500 **c.** 13 months
20. Answers will vary.

9•1 Gathering and Recording Data

1.

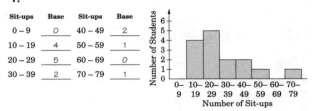

Sit-ups	Base	Sit-ups	Base
0 – 9	O	40 – 49	2
10 – 19	4	50 – 59	1
20 – 29	5	60 – 69	O
30 – 39	2	70 – 79	1

9•2 Using Graphs and Tables

1. 559,000 more dairy cows than sheep
3. 68,531,000 **5.** $12.50

9•3 Using Bar, Line, and Circle Graphs

1. January, March, November; these are winter months when the heat is used.
3. $3,000 **5.** 65% **7.** 5 P.M.

9•4 Finding the Mean, Median, and Mode

1. Mean: 38; Median: 36; Mode: 36

3. Mean: 3.2; Median: 3.5; Mode: 4

5. Mean: $2.27; Median: $2.25; Mode: $2.25

9•5 Finding Probability

1. Yes

3. $P(\text{yellow}) = \frac{2}{10} = 0.2$

5. $P(\text{orange}) = 0$

7. $P(\text{A or E}) = \frac{2}{6} = \frac{1}{3} \approx 0.33$

9. $P(\text{letter before G}) = 1$

11. $P(\text{number greater than 4}) = \frac{2}{6} = \frac{1}{3} \approx 0.33$

13. $P(12) = 0$

15. a. $P(\text{nickel}) = \frac{23}{50} = 0.46$ **b.** $P(\text{dime}) = \frac{17}{50} = 0.34$
   c. $P(\text{quarter}) = \frac{6}{50} = 0.12$ **d.** $P(\text{penny}) = \frac{4}{50} = 0.08$

17. $\frac{15}{20} = \frac{3}{4} = 0.75$

Chapter 9 Review

1. frequency   **2.** mean   **3.** mode   **4.** line graph

5. all possible outcomes

6.

S:	3
M:	7
L:	6

7.

Height of plant after two weeks	Number of plants
0 – 1 cm:	1
1 – 2 cm:	3
2 – 3 cm:	4
3 – 4 cm:	2

8.

T-Shirt size	Number sold
S:	3
M:	7
L:	6

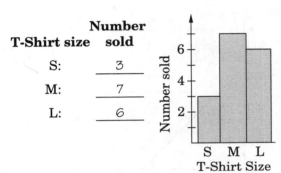

9. $4,000   **10.** $13,000   **11.** 85°F   **12.** Noon–2 P.M.

13. 52.4%   **14.** 36.852 million = 36,852,000

15. Mean: 90.6; Median: 90; Mode: None

16. Mean: 3.625; Median: 2; Mode: 2

17. $P(\text{imperfect}) = \frac{450}{12,000} = 0.0375$

18. $P(\text{less than 5}) = \frac{4}{6} = \frac{2}{3} \approx 0.67$